Contents

Summary

In most years, the Department of Defense (DoD) provides a five-year plan, called the Future Years Defense Program (FYDP), associated with the budget that it submits to the Congress. Because decisions made in the near term can have consequences for the defense budget well beyond that period, the Congressional Budget Office (CBO) regularly examines DoD's FYDP and projects its budgetary impact roughly a decade beyond the period covered by the FYDP. For this analysis, CBO used the FYDP that was provided to the Congress in April 2013; that FYDP spans fiscal years 2014 to 2018, and CBO's projections span the years 2014 to 2028.

For fiscal year 2014, DoD requested appropriations totaling $607 billion. Of that amount, $527 billion was to fund the "base" programs that constitute the department's normal activities, such as the development and procurement of weapon systems and the day-to-day operations of the military and civilian workforce. The remaining $79 billion was requested to pay for what are termed overseas contingency operations (OCO)—the war in Afghanistan and other nonroutine military activities elsewhere. The FYDP describes DoD's plans for its normal activities and therefore generally corresponds to the base budget. DoD's 2014 plans are similar to its 2013 plans.

CBO produced two projections of the base-budget costs of DoD's plans (expressed in terms of total obligational authority for each fiscal year) as reflected in the FYDP and other long-term planning documents released by DoD.[1] The "CBO projection" uses CBO's estimates of the costs of military activities and the extent to which those costs will change over time; those estimates reflect DoD's experience in recent years. For comparison, the "extension of the FYDP" starts with DoD's estimates of the costs of its plans through 2018 and extends them beyond 2018 using DoD's estimates if available and CBO's projections of price and compensation trends for the overall economy if DoD's estimates are not available. Neither projection should be viewed as a prediction of future funding for DoD's activities; rather, the projections are estimates of the costs of executing the department's current plans without changes.

Under either projection, the costs of DoD's plans would rise steadily over time. In addition, those costs would significantly exceed the limits on budget authority established by the automatic enforcement provisions of the Budget Control Act of 2011, as amended by the American Taxpayer Relief Act of 2012—hereafter referred to collectively as the Budget Control Act (BCA)—for all remaining years subject to those limits (2014 through 2021). To close that gap, which CBO estimates will average between about $60 billion and about $90 billion per year, DoD would have to make sharp cuts to the size of its forces, the development and purchase of weapons, the extent of its operations and training, or some combination of the three.

The CBO Projection Shows That the Cost of DoD's Plans Would Increase Over Time

The costs to implement DoD's 2014 plans would increase over the next 15 years. Under the CBO projection, after adjusting for inflation, the annual cost of the plans would grow from $534 billion in 2014 to $559 billion in 2018 and $615 billion in 2028, for an average

---

1. CBO used total obligational authority (TOA) for this analysis because the FYDP is presented in terms of TOA. Discretionary budget authority, which CBO focuses on in other contexts, usually differs only slightly from TOA in the budget year and is almost identical to TOA in the years beyond the budget year. For example, in discretionary budget authority, DoD's request for 2014 was $606 billion, compared with $607 billion in TOA.

Summary Figure 1.

Costs of DoD's Plans

(Billions of 2014 dollars)

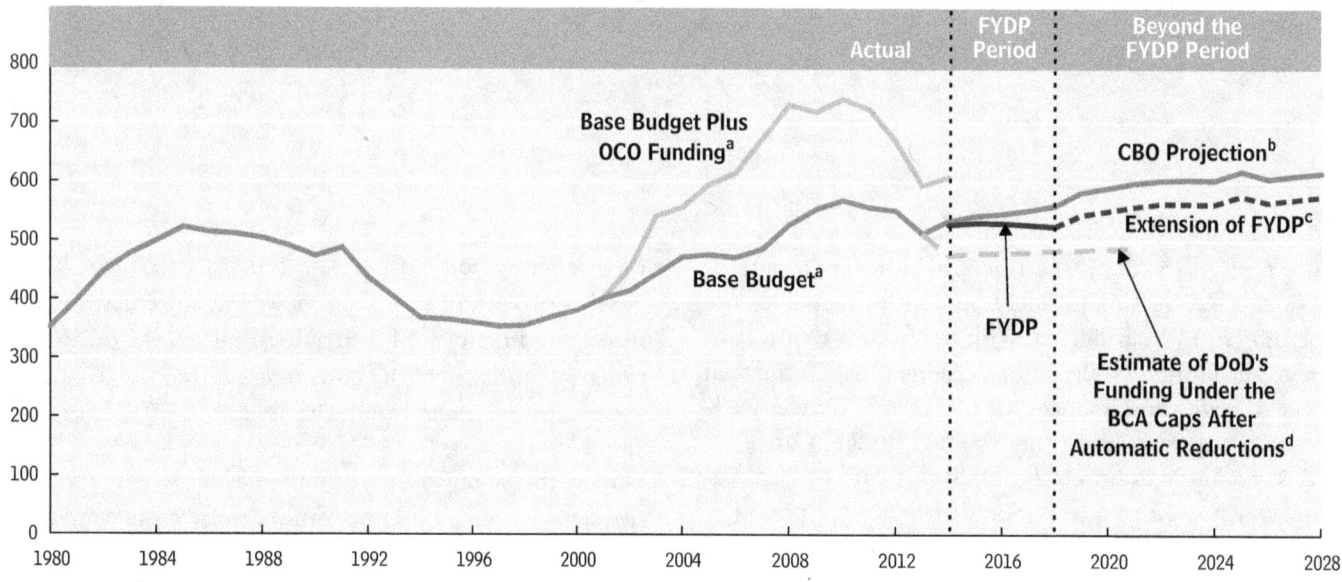

Source: Congressional Budget Office.

Note: DoD = Department of Defense; OCO = overseas contingency operations; FYDP = Future Years Defense Program; FYDP period = 2014 through 2018, the period for which DoD's plans are fully specified; BCA = Budget Control Act of 2011.

a.   Base-budget data include supplemental and emergency funding before 2002. For 2002 to 2014, supplemental and emergency funding for overseas contingency operations, such as those in Afghanistan and Iraq, and for other purposes is shown separately from the base-budget data. No OCO funding is shown for 2015 and later.

b.   The CBO projection of the base budget incorporates costs that are consistent with DoD's recent experience.

c.   For the extension of the FYDP (2019 to 2028), CBO projects the costs of DoD's plans using the department's estimates of costs to the extent they are available and costs that are consistent with CBO's projections of price and compensation trends in the overall economy when the department's estimates are not available.

d.   This estimate assumes that DoD would receive 95.5 percent of the funding limit for national defense after reductions resulting from the BCA's automatic enforcement procedures, which corresponds to DoD's average share of that funding in base budgets from 2002 to 2011.

annual growth rate of 1.0 percent from 2014 to 2028 (see Summary Figure 1). The projected growth in the costs of DoD's plans over the next fifteen years can be attributed to two main factors:

■ The rising costs of operation and support (O&S), which accounts for 67 percent of the cost to implement DoD's plans in 2014, resulting from significant increases in the costs of military health care, compensation of the department's military and civilian employees, and various operation and maintenance activities. After adjusting for inflation, O&S costs would rise by 1.2 percent a year between 2014 and 2028, CBO projects.

■ The rising costs of replacing and modernizing weapon systems, which accounts for 31 percent of the cost to implement DoD's plans in 2014. CBO projects that, after adjusting for inflation, the costs of such activities would rise by 3.0 percent a year between 2014 and 2021, remain at about the 2021 level through 2025, and then decrease through 2028.

According to the CBO projection, the average costs of DoD's base-budget plans from 2014 through 2018 would exceed average spending for DoD from 1980 to 2012 by about $90 billion a year after adjusting for inflation. Moreover, the average costs of DoD's plans from 2014 through 2028 would exceed the 1980–2012 average by about $130 billion a year after adjusting for inflation.

The growth in DoD's costs over time would be slower than CBO's projection of the growth of the U.S. economy, so costs would decline as a share of gross domestic product (GDP). Spending for DoD's base budget was 3.1 percent of GDP in 2012 and would decline to 2.7 percent of GDP in 2018 and to 2.5 percent in 2028, according to the CBO projection of the costs of DoD's plans.

Costs Would Increase Less Under the Extension of the FYDP Than Under the CBO Projection

CBO compared its projection of the costs of DoD's plans with a projection based on DoD's estimate of the costs of its plans through 2018 and an extension of those estimates through 2028. That extension is based on DoD's estimates of costs beyond 2018 if they are available (for instance, for some weapon systems) and on costs consistent with CBO's projections of price and compensation trends for the overall economy if estimates by the department are not available (for instance, for health care costs and pay). For most categories of DoD's budget, costs under the CBO projection are higher than the costs estimated by DoD in the FYDP and the extrapolated costs for the extension of the FYDP. In particular, DoD's costs of providing health care and of developing and buying weapons, which CBO uses in constructing its projection of the costs of DoD's plans, have historically been higher than the department's planning estimates, which DoD incorporates in the FYDP and CBO extrapolates for the FYDP extension.

CBO's analysis yields three conclusions:

■ Using DoD's estimates of costs and CBO's extension of those estimates, the department would need $527 billion in 2014 to execute its base budget. Costs would then edge down, to $524 billion by 2018 after adjusting for inflation, before rising again, to $575 billion in 2028. Between 2014 and 2028, costs would grow at an average annual rate of 0.6 percent after adjusting for inflation.

■ DoD's estimate of the cumulative cost of its plans over the 2014–2018 period is 3.4 percent lower than the CBO projection, an average of $19 billion less per year after adjusting for inflation. The cumulative cost of DoD's plans through 2028 (using DoD's estimates

and CBO's extension of the FYDP) is 5.6 percent lower than the CBO projection, an average of $33 billion less per year.

■ DoD's estimate of the cost of its base budget in 2014 is $7 billion less than CBO's estimate for two reasons. First, CBO includes the cost of all active-duty personnel, whereas DoD proposes to shift the cost of some of those personnel (including not only their pay but also some other costs to support those personnel) to the OCO budget. Second, CBO assumes that the Congress will continue its history of rejecting many of DoD's proposals to shift some health care costs to the military beneficiaries receiving the care.

The Costs of DoD's Plans Greatly Exceed the Limits Established by the Budget Control Act

CBO compared both projections of the costs of executing DoD's plans with the funding that could be provided to the department under the BCA, which limits discretionary appropriations through 2021. If DoD continues to receive its historical share of the national defense budget, CBO's analysis yields these four conclusions:[2]

■ Under the CBO projection, the cumulative cost of DoD's base-budget plans for 2014 through 2021 would be $701 billion, or about $88 billion a year, higher (in nominal terms) than the funding that would be provided to DoD under the limits set by the BCA's automatic enforcement procedures. (That gap would be $645 billion after adjusting for inflation.)

■ If the automatic reductions were repealed and the original caps on funding established by the BCA were restored, the cumulative cost of DoD's base-budget plans under the CBO projection for 2014 through 2021 would be $283 billion higher (in nominal terms) than the funding that would be provided to DoD.

---

2. The Budget Control Act limits budget authority for national defense (budget function 050), not DoD (budget subfunction 051). Since 2001, DoD has received an average of 95.5 percent of the budget authority for national defense. CBO estimated DoD's future share of the limits on national defense funding assuming that the department would continue to receive that historical share.

(That gap would be $256 billion after adjusting for inflation.)

■ Under the FYDP and its extension, the cumulative cost (in nominal terms) of DoD's plans for 2014 through 2021 would be $471 billion, or about $59 billion a year, higher than would be available under the BCA's automatic enforcement procedures and $7 billion higher per year than would be available under the original caps.

■ Even with the BCA's automatic enforcement procedures in effect, DoD's base budget in 2014 would be larger than it was in 2006 (in 2014 dollars) and larger than the average base budget during the 1980s, a decade that included a large military buildup (see Summary Figure 1). After 2014, the BCA will allow the base budget to grow very slowly in real terms through 2021.

How the automatic enforcement provisions of the BCA would affect DoD's budget in 2014 depends on how much the Congress appropriates for the department. If the Congress appropriates no more for DoD's base budget than the amount permitted under the BCA, there would be no sequestration (the cancellation of budgetary resources after they have been appropriated), and any funding provided for overseas contingency operations would not be affected. However, if the Congress appropriates more than the BCA allows, the difference between the appropriated amount and the BCA limit would be subject to sequestration, as it was in 2013; in that case, funding for overseas contingency operations could also be cut. Those same procedures would apply in subsequent years through 2021.

CBO's Projections of the Cost of DoD's Plans

The federal government's fiscal pressures have increased scrutiny of the Department of Defense's (DoD's) budget. Although funding decisions are usually made on an annual basis, near-term decisions about issues such as pay raises, health benefits for military retirees, and the acquisition of weapon systems can have effects on the composition and costs of the nation's armed forces that last many years.

To provide information about its plans beyond the coming year, DoD usually issues a Future Years Defense Program (FYDP) in conjunction with its annual budget request. The FYDP is a detailed description of DoD's plans and the costs of those plans over the next five years. The latest FYDP, which was issued in April 2013, covers fiscal years 2014 to 2018.

Although DoD publishes information about its longer-term plans for some activities, such as shipbuilding and aircraft procurement, details about most activities beyond the FYDP period are unspecified. To gain a more complete picture of the funding that would be needed for DoD's current plans over the longer term, the Congressional Budget Office (CBO) has projected the costs of DoD's plans over the next 15 years, through 2028. This study presents the results of those projections.

DoD's Budget Request

The FYDP and CBO's projections begin with DoD's proposed budget for 2014, in which the department requested a total of $607 billion in new funding.[1] That request can be separated into two parts:

■ $527 billion for the base budget, which funds the normal activities of the department, including manning and training the force, developing and procuring weapon systems, and the day-to-day operations of the military and civilian workforce, and

■ $79 billion for overseas contingency operations (OCO), which refer to the war in Afghanistan and other nonroutine military activities elsewhere.

CBO's analysis focuses on DoD's base budget. Although OCO funding has accounted for a significant fraction of DoD's total spending over the past 12 years, future spending for such operations will depend on how conditions evolve in Afghanistan and on whether new contingencies or wars arise overseas.

The request for DoD's base budget in 2014 is, after accounting for inflation, one percent less than the amount that the Administration requested for 2013. However, if DoD continued to receive its historical share of the national defense budget, the 2014 request would be 11 percent more than what would be available to DoD given the limit on discretionary funding for national defense established under the automatic enforcement provisions of the Budget Control Act of 2011 as modified by the American Taxpayer Relief Act of 2012 (Public Laws 112-25 and 112-240, respectively, and hereafter referred to collectively as the BCA). The implications of the BCA for DoD's funding are discussed later in this chapter.

---

1. Unless otherwise noted, all costs in this study apply to fiscal years and are expressed in fiscal year 2014 dollars of total obligational authority (TOA). Whereas discretionary budget authority describes the authority provided by an appropriation act to incur financial obligations, TOA is a term used by DoD to measure the funding available for its programs. TOA differs from discretionary budget authority principally in that it adjusts for the spending of some receipts and for the timing of cancellations of prior-year budget authority. In recent years, the difference between TOA and discretionary budget authority in DoD's budget request for the coming year has generally been $3 billion or less. After 2014, TOA and budget discretionary authority are almost identical through the FYDP period.

Figure 1-1.

Costs of DoD's Plans, by Appropriation Category

(Billions of 2014 dollars)

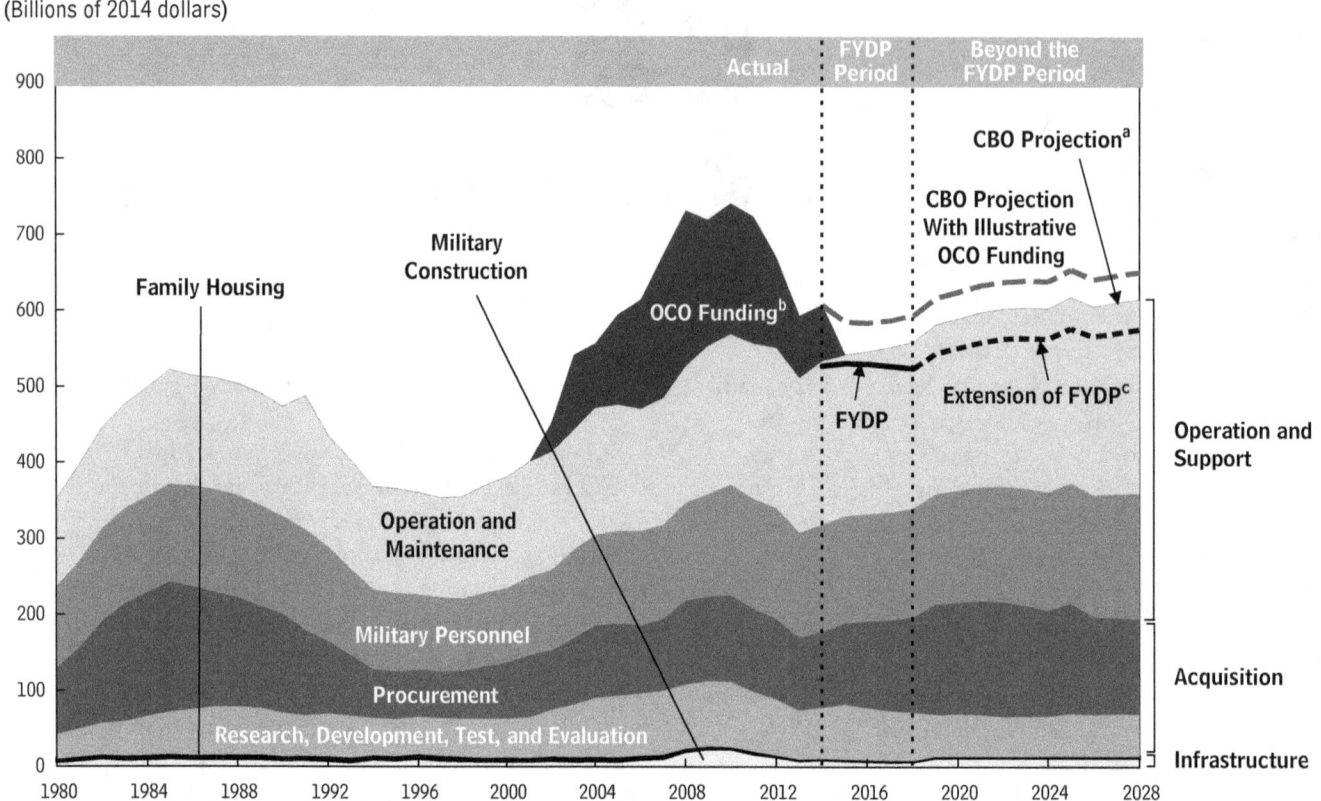

Source: Congressional Budget Office.

Notes: The amounts shown for the Future Years Defense Program (FYDP) and the extension of the FYDP are totals for all categories.

     DoD = Department of Defense; OCO = overseas contingency operations; FYDP period = 2014 through 2018, the period for which DoD's plans are fully specified.

a.   Each category shows the CBO projection of the base budget from 2014 to 2028. That projection incorporates costs that are consistent with DoD's recent experience.

b.   Base-budget data include supplemental and emergency funding before 2002. For 2002 and later, supplemental and emergency funding for overseas contingency operations, such as those in Afghanistan and Iraq, and for other purposes is shown separately from the base-budget data.

c.   For the extension of the FYDP (2019 to 2028), CBO projects the costs of DoD's plans using the department's estimates of costs to the extent they are available and costs that are consistent with CBO's projections of price and compensation trends in the overall economy when the department's estimates are not available.

Nearly all of DoD's funding for its base budget is provided in six appropriation categories (see Figure 1-1). In its analysis of the costs of DoD's plans, CBO organized those six categories into three broader groups: operation and support (O&S), acquisition, and infrastructure.

Operation and support includes appropriations for operation and maintenance (O&M) and for military personnel. O&M appropriations fund most of the day-to-day operations of the military, the maintenance of equipment, the purchase of spare parts, the training of

military units, the majority of costs of the military's health care program, compensation for most of DoD's civilian employees, and payments to DoD's support contractors. Military personnel accounts fund compensation for uniformed service members, including pay, housing and food allowances, and related items, such as moving service members and their families to new duty stations. O&M represents the largest portion, nearly 40 percent, of the request for the base budget in 2014, followed by military personnel, at 26 percent.

Acquisition includes procurement and research, development, test, and evaluation (RDT&E). Procurement accounts fund the purchase of new weapon systems and other major equipment, as well as upgrades to existing weapon systems. RDT&E accounts pay for the development of technology and weapons. Procurement represents 19 percent of the request for the base budget in 2014; and RDT&E, 13 percent.

Infrastructure refers to construction at DoD facilities. Appropriations for military construction and family housing fund the construction of buildings and housing on military installations. Together, they make up the remaining 2 percent of the request for the base budget.

CBO's Approach for the Projections

This study provides CBO's independent projections of the costs of implementing DoD's plans for operation and support, acquisition, and infrastructure contained in the 2014 FYDP. Extrapolating from the 2014–2018 period covered by those plans, CBO projects costs (in terms of total obligational authority) through 2028. In making its projections, CBO relied on the number of military personnel, acquisition plans, and policies spelled out in the 2014 FYDP and the long-term acquisition plans that DoD publishes in selected acquisition reports and other official documents, such as the Navy's 30-year shipbuilding plan and DoD's 30-year aviation plan.[2] For the years beyond 2018, CBO assumed that the force structure and number of military and civilian personnel planned by DoD for 2018 would remain unchanged.

CBO made two projections of the costs of DoD's plans:

■ The "CBO projection," which covers the period from 2014 to 2028 and is based on CBO's estimates of future costs, and

■ The "extension of the FYDP," which covers the period from 2019 to 2028 and is based on DoD's estimates of costs if they are available and costs that are consistent

with CBO's projections of price and compensation trends in the overall economy if DoD's estimates are not available.

The CBO projection uses CBO's estimates of the costs of military activities and the extent to which those costs would change over time; those estimates reflect DoD's experience in recent years (see Table 1-1 for details). CBO's projection of the base budget includes the costs of all active-duty personnel, although DoD plans to fund some of those personnel out of the budget for overseas contingency operations. Also, the CBO projection does not include savings starting in 2014 related to several Administration policy proposals for providing health care because the Congress has, historically, resisted DoD's requests to increase the share of health care costs paid by the people receiving that care. Because of those differences, the CBO projection for the base budget in 2014 is about one percent higher than DoD's request.

For the extension of the FYDP, CBO used DoD's estimates of costs for 2014 through 2018. For 2019 through 2028, CBO projected the costs of DoD's plans using the department's estimates of longer-term costs if they were available (for some major weapon systems, for instance) and costs that were consistent with CBO's projections of price and compensation trends in the U.S. economy if estimates by the department were not available (for health care costs and pay for military and civilian personnel, for instance; see Table 1-1 for details).

For most categories of DoD's plans, costs in the CBO projection are higher than the costs estimated by DoD in the FYDP and the assumed costs for the extension of the FYDP. In particular, during the past several decades, the costs of developing and buying weapons have been, on average, 20 percent to 30 percent higher than the department's initial estimates. DoD and the Congress have made some changes to the way that weapon systems are developed and purchased, but it is not yet clear whether those efforts will lower the growth in costs below historical averages.

The two projections are not predictions of future funding for DoD; rather, they are estimates of the costs of executing the department's current plans. Defense plans can be affected by unpredicted changes in the international security environment, decisions made by the Congress, and other factors that could result in substantial departures from the department's current intentions. One such

---

2. If a weapon system reaches the end of its service life before 2028 and DoD has not planned a replacement system, CBO assumes that the department will develop and purchase a new system to replace the aging one. DoD has not published plans for minor procurement programs extending beyond the FYDP period. Therefore, CBO estimated costs for those programs on the basis of historical correlations between funding for major and minor programs.

Table 1-1.

Cost Assumptions for CBO's Two Projections of DoD's Plans

	CBO Projection (2014 to 2028)	Extension of FYDP[a] (2019 to 2028)
Military Pay	1.0% increase in 2014; ECI after 2014	ECI[b]
Civilian Pay	1.0% increase in 2014; ECI after 2014	ECI[b]
Military Health Care	DoD's estimates through 2018, excluding savings from cost-sharing proposals that the Congress has historically rejected, plus growth of 1.0% per year in the cost of direct (in-house) medical care; after 2018, tracks CBO's projection of growth rates for health care spending nationally	Tracks CBO's projection of growth rates for health care spending nationally
Operating Forces	DoD's estimates through 2018, plus the costs (including O&M) of the active-duty manpower that DoD funds with the OCO budget; after 2018, costs aside from civilian pay and military health care grow at the historical average rate	Costs aside from civilian pay and military health care grow at the historical average rate
Acquisition	Historical average cost growth	DoD's estimates with no cost growth
Military Construction and Family Housing	DoD's estimates through 2018; no real (inflation-adjusted) growth beyond 2018	No real growth

Source: Congressional Budget Office.

Note: DoD = Department of Defense; FYDP = Future Years Defense Program; ECI = employment cost index for wages and salaries in the private sector, as reported by the Bureau of Labor Statistics; O&M = operation and maintenance; OCO = overseas contingency operations.

a.   The extension of the FYDP uses the cost estimates provided in the Future Years Defense Program through 2018.

b.   Military and civilian pay would increase with the ECI starting in 2019 but from a lower level than in CBO's projections because DoD projects smaller pay raises during the 2014–2018 period.

factor is that DoD and the Congress frequently respond to higher-than-expected costs of weapon systems by changing acquisition plans—for example, delaying or reducing purchases of weapon systems or canceling systems outright. Another increasingly prominent factor is the growing pressure on the federal budget as a whole. The Budget Control Act limits DoD's funding to amounts that are well below the costs of implementing the department's plans, according to both CBO's and DoD's estimates.

Projections of Costs

CBO's projections include the costs of DoD's base-budget plans over two time spans: the period from 2014 to 2018, which is covered by the FYDP, and the period from 2019 to 2028. Because the amount and

composition of funding that will be requested for future overseas contingency operations are uncertain, costs for them are projected only as illustrative totals and are not broken out by budget category.

Costs of DoD's Plans During the FYDP Period (2014 to 2018)

According to the CBO projection, the annual cost of carrying out DoD's plans would rise from $534 billion in 2014 to $559 billion in real (inflation-adjusted) terms by 2018—an average increase of 1.1 percent per year (see Table 1-2). In contrast, DoD's estimates in the FYDP anticipate that carrying out the department's plans would leave the base budget essentially unchanged (in real terms) between 2014 and 2018. Those estimates show costs of $524 billion in 2018, although they would be

Table 1-2.

Historical Costs and CBO's Projection of Costs of DoD's Plans in Selected Years

(Billions of 2014 dollars)

	2001	2012	FYDP Period 2014	FYDP Period 2018	Beyond the FYDP Period 2023	Beyond the FYDP Period 2028	Average, 2014–2028
			Base Budget				
Operation and Support							
Operation and maintenance[a]	150	211	215	218	237	256	231
Military personnel	103	146	141	143	154	165	151
Subtotal	254	356	356 [b]	361	391	421	382
Acquisition							
Procurement	82	106	99	125	146	125	131
Research, development, test, and evaluation	54	74	68	64	53	56	59
Subtotal	136	180	167	189	199	181	190
Infrastructure							
Military construction	7	13	9	7	12	12	11
Family housing	5	2	2	1	1	1	1
Subtotal	12	15	11	8	14	14	12
Total Base Budget	**401**	**551**	**534**	**559**	**604**	**615**	**584**
			Supplemental and Emergency Funding for Overseas Contingency Operations				
Total OCO Funding	n.a.	119	74 [b]	n.a.	n.a.	n.a.	n.a.
			Total				
Total DoD Budget	**401**	**670**	**608**	n.a.	n.a.	n.a.	n.a.

Source: Congressional Budget Office.

Notes: The CBO projection incorporates costs that are consistent with the Department of Defense's (DoD's) recent experience.

FYDP = Future Years Defense Program; FYDP period = 2014 through 2018, the period for which DoD's plans are fully specified; OCO = overseas contingency operations; n.a. = not applicable.

a. For this analysis, CBO folded appropriations for most revolving funds (such as the one for the Defense Commissary Agency) into the appropriations for operation and maintenance. CBO treated as acquisition the accounts in the National Defense Sealift Fund that are used to purchase ships.

b. For 2014, CBO shifted $3.5 billion in the military personnel account and $2.1 billion in the operation and maintenance account from the OCO budget into the base budget to fund 38,100 active-duty soldiers and marines that DoD plans to fund out of the OCO budget. DoD requested a total of $79 billion for the OCO budget.

slightly (less than 1 percent) higher for 2015 through 2017 (see Table 1-3).

Cumulative costs for 2014 through 2018 under the CBO projection are $2,732 billion, some 4 percent greater than costs under DoD's estimates. Most of that difference results from CBO's higher estimates of the cost to pay military and civilian personnel, develop and procure new

weapon systems, and provide health care to service members and retirees and their families. Much of the remaining difference is attributable to CBO's decision to include in the base budget the military personnel costs and some O&M costs for 38,100 active-duty soldiers and marines that DoD plans to fund out of its budget for contingency operations in 2014 and smaller numbers

Table 1-3.

Comparison of the CBO Projection of DoD's Future Years Defense Program and DoD's Own Projection

(Billions of 2014 dollars)

		FYDP Period					
	2013	**Budget Request, 2014**	**2015**	**2016**	**2017**	**2018**	**Total, 2014– 2018**
CBO Projection, Base Budget	512	534	542	546	552	559	2,732
DoD's 2014 FYDP, Base Budget	512	527	530	530	527	524	2,639
Difference Between the CBO Projection and DoD's FYDP	0	7	12	16	24	34	93

Source: Congressional Budget Office.

Notes: The CBO projection incorporates costs that are consistent with the Department of Defense's (DoD's) recent experience.

　　　FYDP = Future Years Defense Program; FYDP period = 2014 through 2018, the period for which DoD's plans are fully specified.

of such personnel from 2015 through 2017.[3] In DoD's plans, the costs of personnel funded outside the base budget would amount to almost $6 billion in 2014 but would decline to zero by the end of 2017 as the size of military forces is reduced.

Costs of DoD's Plans Beyond the FYDP Period (2019 Through 2028)

According to the CBO projection, the annual cost (in 2014 dollars) of carrying out DoD's plans would rise from $559 billion in 2018 to $615 billion in 2028 (see Table 1-2). Between 2018 and 2028, the average real increase in costs would be 1.0 percent per year. That increase can be explained by rising costs of operation and maintenance and of pay and benefits for military service members; acquisition costs would be slightly lower in 2028 than in 2018, although they would be higher in many of the intervening years (see Figure 1-2).

Costs for O&M are projected to grow by an average of 1.6 percent per year, from $218 billion in 2018 to

---

3. In the past, only the incremental cost of deploying an active-duty service member to a contingency operation has been included in the OCO budget. For example, base pay and normal peacetime allowances for a deployed service member would be funded from the base budget, but combat pay would be funded from the OCO budget. Beginning in 2013, however, DoD has shifted to the OCO budget the entire cost for the number of service members above the number slated to remain in 2017, the end of the planned force drawdown. See Box 2-1 on page 18 for additional details.

$256 billion in 2028, after adjusting for inflation. That growth would result from the rising costs of medical care for military personnel and their families, of pay and benefits for civilian workers, and of maintaining equipment. Appropriations for military personnel would increase by about 1.4 percent per year from $143 billion in 2018 to $165 billion in 2028, reflecting pay raises exceeding the rate of inflation.

After a rapid increase over the next eight years, the total costs of developing and purchasing new weapon systems and upgrading older systems under DoD's current plans would peak at $205 billion in 2021. Acquisition costs would gradually decline thereafter, to $181 billion in 2028. In those later years, the department would have largely achieved its current modernization goals, and it has not articulated plans for the next round of modernization. The decline might not occur if DoD initiated new modernization programs that are not anticipated in CBO's projections.

The costs of DoD's plans would be lower than the CBO projection if the Congress adopts DoD's proposals to increase cost sharing for users of the military health system and to raise pay for military personnel and civilians more slowly between 2014 and 2018 than is specified in current law, and if DoD is able to rein in the growth in the cost of weapon systems or operations. Projected costs under the extension of the FYDP, which incorporates those alternative policies and assumptions, would reach $575 billion by 2028—about $40 billion, or 7 percent, less than the amount in the CBO projection.

Figure 1-2.

CBO Projection of Base-Budget Costs of DoD's Plans, by Appropriation Category

(Billions of 2014 dollars)

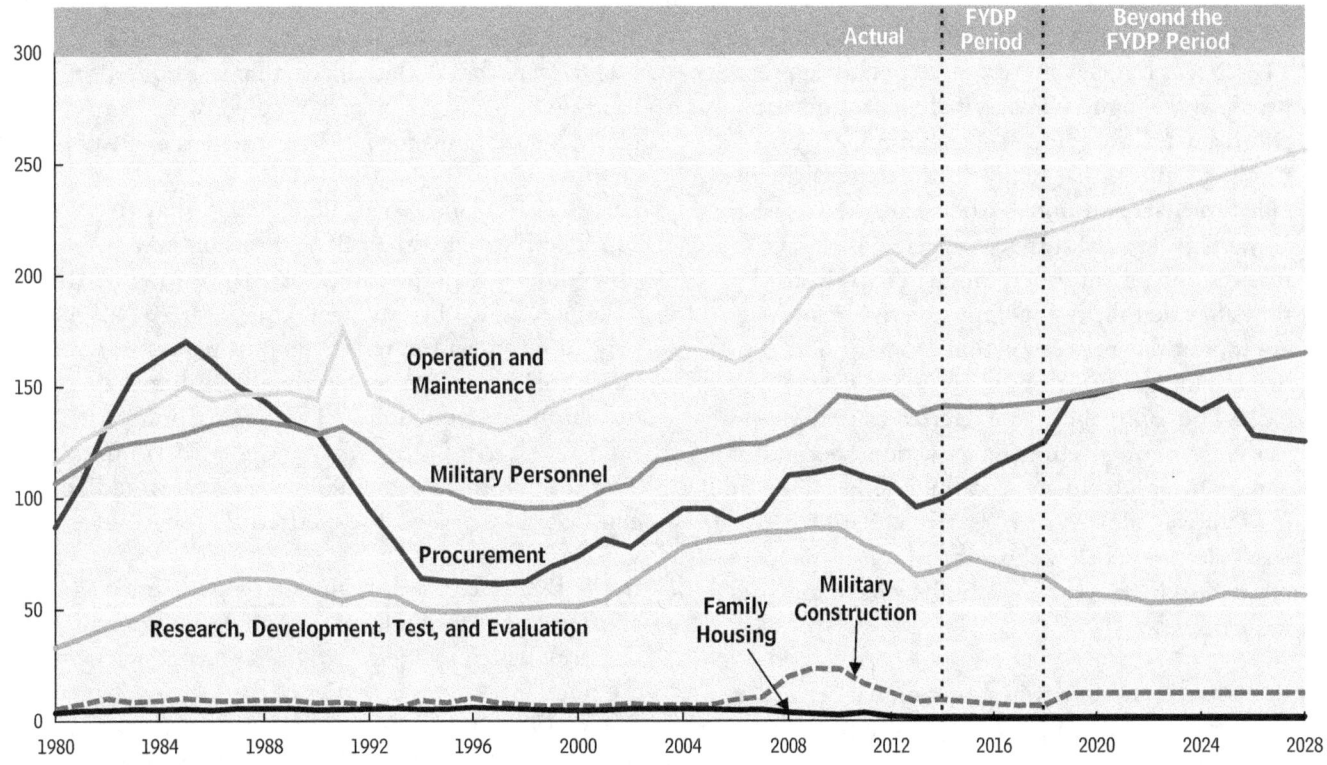

Source: Congressional Budget Office.

Notes: Base-budget data include supplemental and emergency funding before 2002.

DoD = Department of Defense; FYDP = Future Years Defense Program; FYDP period = 2014 through 2018, the period for which DoD's plans are fully specified.

Costs of DoD's Plans in the Context of the Budget Control Act of 2011

The Budget Control Act of 2011 established limits (caps) on discretionary appropriations for national defense through 2021 and also included provisions for automatic reductions to those caps, which are now in effect (see Box 1-1). Under both the CBO projection and the FYDP and extension, the costs of DoD's base-budget plans for 2014 and all other years through 2021 would exceed those caps after automatic reductions (see Figure 1-3). Any amounts that the Congress appropriates above the levels permitted under the BCA would be subject to sequestration (the cancellation of budgetary resources after they have been appropriated). If that occurred, the budget for overseas contingency operations

would also be subject to sequestration, as it was under the sequestration for 2013.

If DoD's base budget continued to receive its historical share of the national defense budget (95.5 percent over the past decade), that base budget would be limited by the BCA to $475 billion for 2014, $59 billion lower than the CBO projection of the cost of DoD's plans for that year. The CBO projection of the cost (in nominal terms) of DoD's plans would exceed the BCA's cumulative limits on funding by $349 billion from 2014 through 2018 and by $351 billion from 2019 through 2021 for a total of $701 billion (see the fifth row in the top panel of Table 1-4 on page 14). Under the FDYP and its extension, the cost (in nominal terms) of DoD's plans would exceed the BCA limits by less than the CBO projection would but still by large amounts: $52 billion in 2014,

Box 1-1.

The Budget Control Act of 2011 and DoD's Budget

The Budget Control Act of 2011 (BCA, Public Law 112-25) set limits (caps) on discretionary appropriations through 2021 and included automatic enforcement procedures—which further reduce funding limits—that took effect because lawmakers failed to enact additional deficit reduction legislation by January 15, 2012. Once triggered, those automatic enforcement procedures had two effects. First, they allocated the overall limits on discretionary appropriations between national defense and non-defense budget functions by setting separate caps for each. Those initial caps are referred to in this report as the caps *before* automatic reductions. Second, the automatic enforcement procedures reduced the funding that was allowed each year from 2013 to 2021 to levels that were below those initial caps, which are referred to here as the BCA limits *after* automatic reductions.[1]

Because the appropriations for national defense for 2013 exceeded the BCA limits after automatic reductions, the funding available to the Department of Defense (DoD) was reduced by canceling a portion of the budgetary resources already provided to that point through an action known as sequestration. For DoD, sequestration in 2013 amounted to $37 billion, $31 billion of which was taken from 2013 appropriations and $6 billion of which was taken from unobligated funds appropriated in earlier years. The lower amount that DoD received after sequestration was insufficient to fully execute its plans for 2013. Consequently, DoD absorbed the cuts from sequestration in 2013 by taking measures such as temporarily grounding some aircraft squadrons, canceling planned training for some ground units, canceling some Navy ship deployments, deferring some acquisition, furloughing most DoD civilians for 6 days, and not renewing some contracts.

Those measures amount to a de facto change in DoD's plans for 2013, a change that was not reflected in its 2014 FYDP because those plans were completed before funds for 2013 were sequestered.

DoD's 2014 plans also assume budgets that are considerably higher than BCA limits on new discretionary appropriations for 2014 through 2018. Although DoD's base-budget request for 2014 is one percent lower (in real terms) than its request for 2013, it is 11 percent higher than BCA limits after the automatic reductions.[2] If Congress appropriates funds in excess of those allowed under BCA limits after the automatic reductions, the excess would be eliminated by means of sequestration.

In the BCA, defense appropriations are defined as appropriations for budget function 050 (national defense), which includes DoD's military activities, the nuclear weapons activities of the Department of Energy (DOE), and the national security activities of several other agencies.[3] On average during the past 10 years, funding for DoD has accounted for 95.5 percent of total funding for budget function 050. For the purpose of portraying BCA limits for DoD alone, the Congressional Budget Office assumed that the department would be allocated that same share of the total discretionary funding for national defense that would be allowed under the BCA's limits. For 2014, the Administration has requested $527 billion for DoD's base budget, about $18 billion for DOE activities, and about $7 billion for other national security activities.

---

1. The American Taxpayer Relief Act of 2012 modified the limits for 2013 and 2014, effectively moving funding forward by increasing the limit for 2013 but decreasing it for 2014. The limits for 2015 through 2021 were unchanged.

2. For more information on those reductions, see Congressional Budget Office, *The Budget and Economic Outlook: Fiscal Years 2012 to 2022* (January 2012), Box 1-2, www.cbo.gov/publication/42905; and *Final Sequestration Report for Fiscal Year 2013* (March 2013), www.cbo.gov/publication/44021.

3. For information about the caps on discretionary budget authority for national defense, see Congressional Budget Office, *Sequestration Update Report: August 2013*, Table 2 (August 2013), www.cbo.gov/publication/44491.

Figure 1-3.

Costs of DoD's Plans in the Context of the Budget Control Act of 2011

(Billions of 2014 dollars)

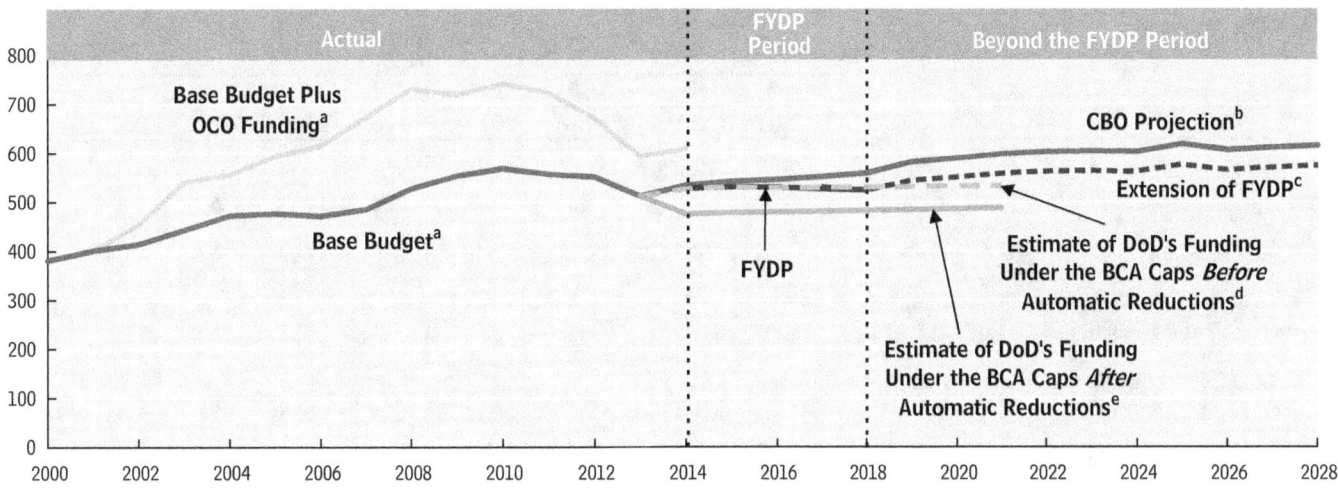

Source: Congressional Budget Office.

Note: DoD = Department of Defense; OCO = overseas contingency operations; FYDP = Future Years Defense Program; FYDP period =
          2014 through 2018, the period for which DoD's plans are fully specified; BCA = Budget Control Act of 2011.

a.   Base-budget data include supplemental and emergency funding before 2002. For 2002 to 2014, supplemental and emergency funding
      for overseas contingency operations, such as those in Afghanistan and Iraq, and for other purposes is shown separately from the base-
      budget data. No OCO funding is shown for 2015 and later.

b.   The CBO projection of the base budget incorporates costs that are consistent with DoD's recent experience.

c.   For the extension of the FYDP (2019 to 2028), CBO projects the costs of DoD's plans using the department's estimates of costs to the
      extent they are available and costs that are consistent with CBO's projections of price and compensation trends in the overall economy
      when the department's estimates are not available.

d.   This estimate assumes that DoD would receive 95.5 percent of the funding limit for national defense *before* reductions resulting from the
      BCA's automatic enforcement procedures, which corresponds to DoD's average share of that funding in base budgets from 2002 to 2011.

e.   This estimate assumes that DoD would receive 95.5 percent of the funding limit for national defense *after* reductions resulting from the
      BCA's automatic enforcement procedures, which corresponds to DoD's average share of that funding in base budgets from 2002 to 2011.

$251 billion over the FYDP period, and $471 billion from 2014 through 2021 (see the bottom row in the top panel of Table 1-4).[4]

Costs of DoD's Plans in a Broader Context

CBO's analysis is intended to highlight the long-term budgetary implications of DoD's plans as specified in the 2014 FYDP; it is not an evaluation of the affordability of those plans or the relationship between those plans and the nation's defense needs. When assessing the

affordability of defense plans, some analysts consider the federal government's overall budget situation, including the costs of other programs and the amount of revenues being collected, while other analysts focus on the share of overall economic output (as measured by gross domestic product, or GDP) that is being used for defense.

Although the spending (outlays) required to execute DoD's base-budget plans would increase under the CBO projection, that increase would not be as rapid as the future growth of the economy that CBO projects, so spending would decline over time as a share of GDP (see Figure 1-4). Historically, spending for DoD as a share of GDP fell from an average of 5.5 percent in the 1980s to 3.7 percent in the 1990s. With supplemental and emergency spending for the wars in Iraq and Afghanistan included, DoD's spending as a share of GDP rose above 4 percent after 2007, peaking at 4.5 percent in 2010.

---

4.   In real terms, the cost of DoD's plans would exceed those lower
      limits on funding by $335 billion from 2014 through 2018 and
      $311 billion from 2019 through 2021—a total of $645 billion—
      according to the CBO projection, and by $242 billion from 2014
      through 2018 and $194 billion from 2019 through 2021—a total
      of $436 billion—according to the FYDP and its extension (see the
      bottom two rows in Table 1-4).

Table 1-4.

Costs of DoD's Plans and DoD's Funding Projected Under the Limits of the Budget Control Act of 2011

(Billions of dollars)

	Budget Control Act								Total, 2014–2021
	FYDP								
	2014	2015	2016	2017	2018	2019	2020	2021	
	Nominal Dollars								
CBO Projection[a]	534	553	568	586	606	644	666	689	4,846
FYDP and Extension[b]	527	541	551	560	569	602	622	643	4,616
Estimate of DoD's Funding Under the BCA Caps *Before* Automatic Reductions[c]	527	541	551	563	576	588	602	615	4,563
Estimate of DoD's Funding Under the BCA Caps *After* Automatic Reductions[d]	475	488	499	511	524	536	549	563	4,145
Cuts to DoD's Plans Needed to Satisfy the BCA After Automatic Reductions									
CBO Projection[a]	59	65	69	75	82	108	117	126	701
FYDP and Extension[b]	52	53	52	49	45	66	73	80	471
	2014 Dollars								
CBO Projection[a]	534	542	546	552	559	581	590	598	4,501
FYDP and Extension[b]	527	530	530	527	524	544	551	558	4,291
Estimate of DoD's Funding Under the BCA Caps *Before* Automatic Reductions[c]	527	531	529	530	531	531	533	533	4,245
Estimate of DoD's Funding Under the BCA Caps *After* Automatic Reductions[d]	475	479	480	481	483	484	486	488	3,856
Cuts to DoD's Plans Needed to Satisfy the BCA After Automatic Reductions									
CBO Projection[a]	59	63	66	71	76	97	104	110	645
FYDP and Extension[b]	52	52	50	46	41	60	65	70	436

Source: Congressional Budget Office.

Note: DoD = Department of Defense; FYDP = Future Years Defense Program; BCA = Budget Control Act of 2011.

a.   The CBO projection of the base budget incorporates costs that are consistent with DoD's recent experience.

b.   For the extension of the FYDP (2019 to 2021), CBO projects the costs of DoD's plans using the department's estimates of costs to the extent they are available and costs that are consistent with CBO's projections of price and compensation trends in the overall economy when the department's estimates are not available.

c.   This estimate assumes that DoD would receive 95.5 percent of the funding limit for national defense *before* reductions resulting from the BCA's automatic enforcement procedures, which corresponds to DoD's average share of that funding in base budgets from 2002 to 2011.

d.   This estimate assumes that DoD would receive 95.5 percent of the funding limit for national defense *after* reductions resulting from the BCA's automatic enforcement procedures, which corresponds to DoD's average share of that funding in base budgets from 2002 to 2011.

According to the CBO projection of the base budget, the cost of DoD's plans would decline from 3.0 percent of GDP in 2014 to 2.7 percent by 2018 and to 2.5 percent by 2028. Any future spending for overseas contingency operations would increase the share of GDP spent on defense above those figures, holding all else equal.

Costs for Overseas Contingency Operations

Operations in Afghanistan and elsewhere overseas are continuing, and those operations, along with any others that might arise, will increase total costs relative to DoD's base budget. From 2001 to 2013, DoD's appropriations for overseas contingency operations totaled $1.58 trillion (in

Figure 1-4.

Costs of DoD's Plans as a Share of Economic Output

(Percentage of gross domestic product)

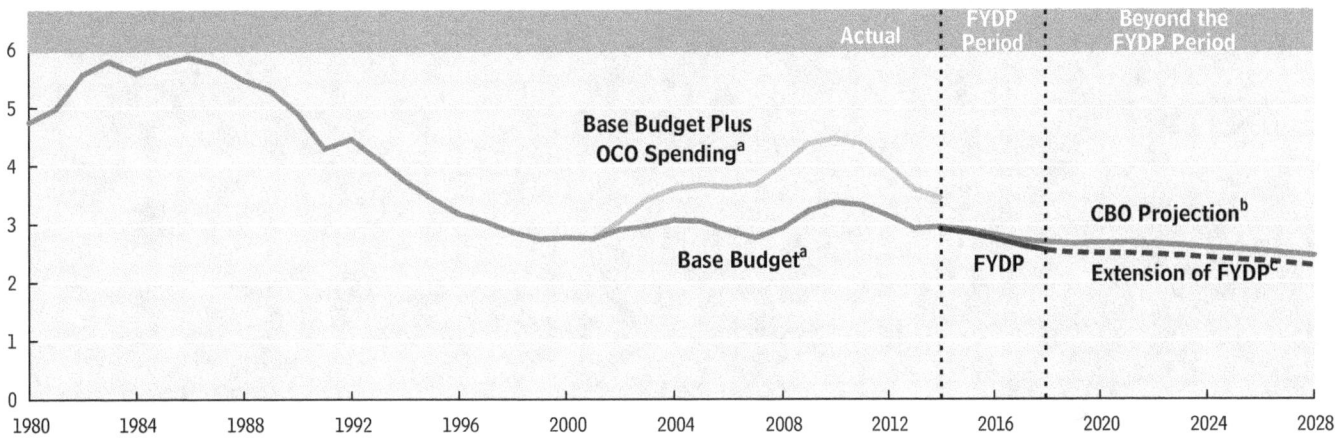

Source: Congressional Budget Office.

Notes: For this figure, estimates describe outlays (as opposed to total obligational authority).

DoD = Department of Defense; FYDP = Future Years Defense Program; OCO = overseas contingency operations; FYDP period = 2014 through 2018, the period for which DoD's plans are fully specified.

a.   Base-budget data include supplemental and emergency funding before 2002. For 2002 to 2014, supplemental and emergency spending for overseas contingency operations, such as those in Afghanistan and Iraq, and for other purposes is shown separately from the base-budget data. No OCO funding is shown for 2015 and later.

b.   The CBO projection of the base budget incorporates costs that are consistent with DoD's recent experience.

c.   For the extension of the FYDP (2019 to 2028), CBO projects the costs of DoD's plans using the department's estimates of costs to the extent they are available and costs that are consistent with CBO's projections of price and compensation trends in the overall economy when the department's estimates are not available.

2014 dollars), an average of about $122 billion per year, or about 20 percent of the department's total funding during that period. Although DoD has requested $79 billion for those purposes for 2014 and some operations are expected to continue after that year, the FYDP does not include estimates of the funding that might be needed to support overseas contingency operations in future years. However, DoD has specified in some of its other budget documents a notional value of $37 billion a year to illustrate the potential implications of OCO funding for its overall budget from 2015 through 2018. Actual amounts requested and appropriated for those years will depend on how overseas operations evolve over time. Funding designated for overseas contingency operations is not constrained by the caps established in the BCA, although it, too, is subject to sequestration if the Congress appropriates more than the BCA limits for the base budget.

The funding needed in the future for overseas contingency operations will depend on how political and military conditions evolve in other countries in the

coming years. As an illustrative example, if today's contingency force was drawn down from the roughly 140,000 troops in December 2012 to 45,000 troops by 2015 and was then maintained at that number through 2028, contingency operations would add a total of about $215 billion above the base budget from 2014 to 2018 for an average of $43 billion per year during that period, and then an average of $36 billion per year thereafter, CBO estimates (see Figure 1-1 on page 6).[5] That overseas force of 45,000 troops would be significantly smaller than the force deployed at the end of 2012 but about three to four times the average number deployed overseas between 1991 and 2001.

---

5.   That scenario for contingency operations is the same as one of the policy alternatives presented in Congressional Budget Office, *The Budget and Economic Outlook: Fiscal Years 2013 to 2023* (February 2013), Table 1-7, www.cbo.gov/publication/43907. The force levels exclude U.S. military personnel who are permanently based overseas (in locations such as South Korea or Okinawa, Japan) but are not engaged in contingency operations. The drawdown through 2015 is roughly consistent with the President's announced plans for decreasing U.S. forces in Afghanistan.

CHAPTER 2

Projections of Operation and Support Costs

For 2014, the Administration requested $349 billion for operation and support—the sum of the appropriations for operation and maintenance and for military personnel (as well as for the Department of Defense's revolving funds, such as the one for the Defense Commissary Agency).[1] That sum represents two-thirds of DoD's total request, excluding funding for overseas contingency operations. The Congressional Budget Office projection for the cost of DoD's plans for operation and support for 2014 is higher—$356 billion—for two reasons: The CBO projection includes costs for active-duty personnel that DoD assumes will be paid for out of funds designated for contingency operations, and it omits savings related to DoD's proposals to shift some health care costs to beneficiaries—proposals that the Congress has historically rejected.

DoD plans to shrink the number of active-duty military personnel by 3 percent between 2014 and 2017 (see Box 2-1). Despite those reductions, operation and support costs would, according to the CBO projection, rise to $361 billion (in 2014 dollars) by 2018 because the costs per person of military and civilian pay, military medical care, and other support would continue to grow over that period as they have in the past (see Figure 2-1 on page 20). In contrast, in the 2014 Future Years Defense Program, DoD estimates that costs for O&S would decline slightly to $342 billion in 2018 . The difference in growth rates stems primarily from CBO's projections of faster growth in the cost of providing medical care to military personnel and their families and higher pay raises for DoD's military personnel and civilian employees.

After 2018—assuming that the numbers of major combat units (Army divisions, Navy ships, Air Force squadrons, and so forth) and personnel remain the same as in 2018—CBO projects that costs (after adjusting for inflation) for O&S would rise steadily to $421 billion by 2028, representing annual growth of about 1.5 percent. As a result, O&S costs would be nearly 20 percent higher in 2028 than in 2014. Such costs would continue to represent about two-thirds of the total cost of DoD's plans. The costs would be lower—$398 billion in 2028—under the extension of the FYDP. From 2019 to 2028, the difference between the two projections for O&S would increase by only a small amount because CBO used identical assumptions for pay raises and the growth in the cost of medical care (see Table 1-1 on page 8).

CBO calculated the future O&S costs of DoD's plans in three parts:

- Compensation for military personnel and DoD's civilian employees (pay, cash benefits, and retirement compensation),

- Medical care for active-duty and retired military personnel and their families, and

- All other categories of operation and maintenance costs (such as fuel, repairs, and spare parts).

Compensation constitutes the largest of the three components in the 2014 budget request, accounting for more than half of the requested appropriation for O&S. Funding for compensation comes from the appropriations for military personnel and for O&M.

Medical care for military personnel, military retirees, and their families is also funded largely from the military personnel and O&M appropriation accounts. Under CBO projection, the cost of such care would grow more quickly than compensation through 2028.

---

1. For this analysis, CBO folded the amounts appropriated for most revolving funds into the appropriation for operation and maintenance. The exception is accounts in the National Defense Sealift Fund that are used to purchase ships, which CBO treated as acquisition.

Box 2-1.

The Number of Military Personnel, 2013 to 2018

Under the Department of Defense's (DoD's) plans, the number of military personnel would decline over the period covered by the Future Years Defense Program (FYDP). DoD measures the size of its force in terms of end strength—the number of military personnel as of the final day of the fiscal year. In 2018, DoD intends to fund end strength of about 1.32 million in the active force, excluding reserve and National Guard personnel on active duty. That total would be about 73,000 fewer than the number serving in 2013; active-duty end strength would fall by about 62,000 in the Army and about 11,000 in the Marine Corps but would be essentially unchanged in the Navy and the Air Force (see the table). The number of service members in the reserve and National Guard would also decline slightly over the FYDP period; DoD plans to fund about 830,000 members in those components in 2018, reflecting a decrease of roughly 12,000 from the number serving in 2013.

Continuing a budgetary practice initiated in 2013, in the 2014 FYDP DoD shifts the costs for the

active-duty personnel that the department plans to eliminate by the end of 2017 from the base budget to the budget for overseas contingency operations (OCO). While last year's OCO budget included only the military personnel costs associated with those personnel, this year's OCO budget also includes some associated operation and maintenance costs. DoD's approach allows the base budget to reflect the operation and support costs of an active-duty force of 1.32 million as early as 2014, even though the actual active-duty force would decline more slowly.

In previous personnel drawdowns, DoD has included the costs for all active-duty personnel in its base budget. Consistent with that earlier practice, the Congressional Budget Office (CBO) shifted all OCO funding for active-duty personnel back into the base budget for the CBO projection. Compared with DoD's plans, that shift resulted in an increase in base-budget costs of $5.6 billion in 2014 and $13 billion from 2014 through 2017.

Continued

The third component includes the purchase through the O&M appropriation of items ranging from office supplies to aircraft fuel, although it excludes major items such as ships, tanks, and aircraft, which are purchased from the procurement accounts. It also includes the purchase of services, such as contracts to maintain facilities, prepare food, repair weapon systems, operate information systems, and conduct many other activities.

CBO estimated costs for compensation and medical care in a "bottom-up" manner by combining estimates of underlying populations, enrollment and participation rates in health care plans, and various factors relating to cost and price. However, such estimates were not possible for the third component of O&S costs because of the wide array of items and services purchased with those funds. Consequently, for that component of O&M, CBO used DoD's estimates through 2018 as a starting point and projected costs from 2019 to 2028 on the basis of DoD's historical experience. (See Box 2-2 on

page 22 for a discussion of how O&M costs have grown over the years.)

Pay, Cash Benefits, and Accrual Payments for Retirement Benefits

Pay and cash benefits for military service members include basic pay, reenlistment bonuses, housing allowances, and various other elements. In addition, DoD's appropriation for military personnel is charged for accrual payments to the Military Retirement Fund; those payments are calculated to provide a balance in the fund that is adequate to pay future retirement benefits to current military personnel. (Health care benefits available to service members and their families through the military medical system are considered in the next section of this chapter.)

The Administration's 2014 budget request includes $204 billion in O&S funding for pay and benefits for DoD's military personnel and most of its civilian

Box 2-1.   Continued

The Number of Military Personnel, 2013 to 2018

DoD's Plans for Active-Duty End Strength

(Thousands of personnel)

	2013	FYDP Period				
	2013	2014	2015	2016	2017	2018
Army						
Base budget	502	490	490	490	490	490
OCO budget	50	30	23	12	0	0
Navy[a]						
Base budget	323	324	323	324	325	326
Marine Corps						
Base budget	182	182	182	182	182	182
OCO budget	11	8	4	0	0	0
Air Force[a]						
Base Budget	329	328	327	327	327	327
DoD Totals						
Base budget	1,337	1,323	1,322	1,323	1,324	1,325
OCO budget	61	38	27	12	0	0
All budgets	1,398	1,361	1,349	1,335	1,324	1,325
Memorandum:						
Cost of Active-Duty Personnel in OCO Budget (Billions of 2014 Dollars)						
Military personnel account	5.6	3.5	2.6	1.6	0.4	0.0
Operation and maintenance account	0	2.1	1.6	1.0	0.3	0.0

Source: Congressional Budget Office.

Notes: The Department of Defense (DoD) measures the size of its force in terms of end strength—the number of military personnel as of the final day of a fiscal year. When estimating the annual costs to fund personnel in the base budget rather than the OCO budget, CBO used the average number of personnel each year.

   FYDP = Future Years Defense Program; OCO = overseas contingency operations.

a.   The Navy and the Air Force do not plan to fund active-duty military end strength with budgets for contingency operations.

employees. About $137 billion of that total is in the military personnel appropriation to support DoD's active-duty service members (plus reserve and National Guard members as necessary), excluding the 38,100 soldiers and marines the department proposes to fund within the overseas contingency operations budget. CBO estimates that an additional $67 billion is in the O&M request to compensate most of DoD's roughly 800,000 full-time-equivalent civilian workers.[2] DoD projects that, over the FYDP period, annual costs to compensate military and civilian personnel will decline to about

$198 billion, reflecting a combination of planned reductions in personnel levels and pay growth below the projected rate of inflation. Under the extension of the

---

2.   Compensation for some civilian employees—about $7 billion in 2014—is paid from other appropriations. For instance, some civilians in military laboratories are paid from the appropriation for research, development, test, and evaluation, and some civilians in acquisition program offices are paid from the appropriation for procurement. See the "Green Book," namely, Department of Defense, *National Defense Budget Estimates for FY 2014*, (May 2013), Tables 6-1, 6-2, and 7-5, http://go.usa.gov/WD5R.

Figure 2-1.

Costs of DoD's Operation and Support Plans

(Billions of 2014 dollars)

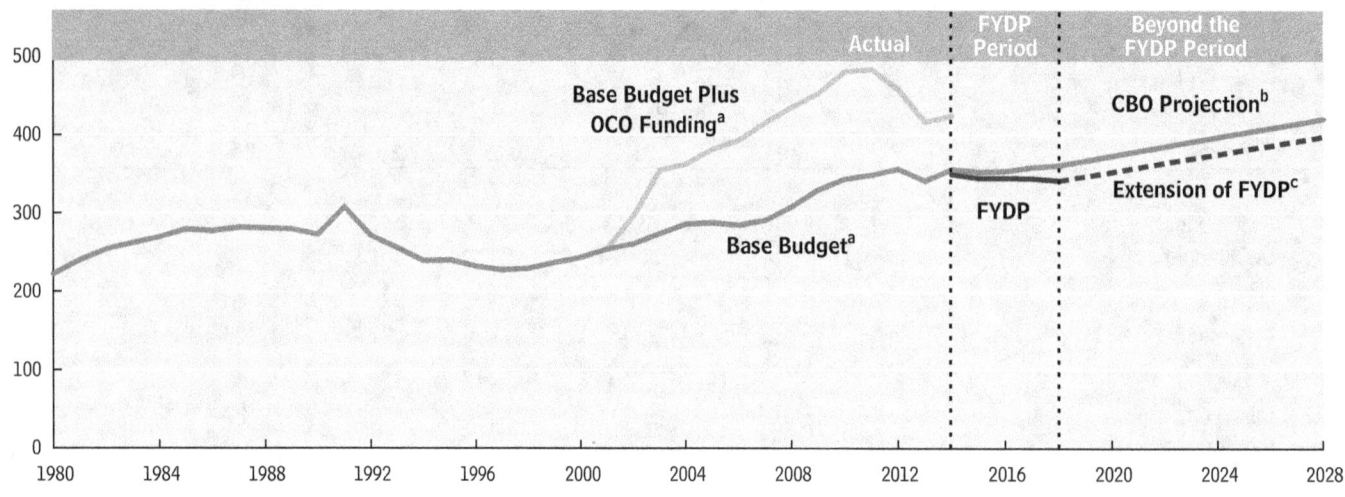

Source: Congressional Budget Office.

Note: DoD = Department of Defense; FYDP = Future Years Defense Program; OCO = overseas contingency operations; FYDP period = 2014 through 2018, the period for which DoD's plans are fully specified.

a.   Base-budget data include supplemental and emergency funding before 2002. For 2002 to 2014, supplemental and emergency funding for overseas contingency operations, such as those in Afghanistan and Iraq, and for other purposes is shown separately from the base-budget data. No OCO funding is shown for 2015 and later.

b.   The CBO projection of the base budget incorporates costs that are consistent with DoD's recent experience.

c.   For the extension of the FYDP (2019 to 2028), CBO projects the costs of DoD's plans using the department's estimates of costs to the extent they are available and costs that are consistent with CBO's projections of price and compensation trends in the overall economy when the department's estimates are not available.

FYDP, those costs would grow by an average of 1.5 percent per year and reach $229 billion in 2028, CBO estimates.

According to the CBO projection of DoD's plans, the costs of pay and benefits in O&S would rise from $208 billion in 2014 to $210 billion in 2018, despite a 3 percent decline in the number of active-duty personnel (see Table 2-1). Those estimates are higher than the costs indicated in the FYDP because CBO assumed that all active-duty service members would be funded within the base budget and that pay raises would be higher than DoD proposes. After 2018, CBO estimates, compensation costs would grow by an average of 1.5 percent per year, reaching $244 billion by 2028.

CBO's projections of real growth in military compensation are based on current law, which indexes the annual increase in basic military pay to the percentage increase in the Bureau of Labor Statistics' employment cost index

(ECI) for wages and salaries in private industry.[3] From 1981 to 2012, the ECI grew more rapidly than the gross domestic product deflator (a measure of the prices of all final goods and services produced in the economy) in all but three of those years.[4] By CBO's estimates, the same pattern will continue between 2014 and 2018, and growth of the ECI will exceed growth of the GDP deflator by an average of 1.7 percentage points per year.[5]

---

3.   37 U.S.C. 1009 (adjustments of monthly basic pay) states that the percentage increase in basic pay for a given calendar year is equal to the percentage increase in the ECI from the third calendar quarter three years prior to the effective date of the pay raise to the third calendar quarter two years prior to the effective date.

4.   This comparison is based on the revised historical data measuring gross domestic product, released in July 2013 by the Bureau of Economic Analysis of the Department of Commerce.

5.   See Congressional Budget Office, *The Budget and Economic Outlook: Fiscal Years 2013 to 2023* (February 2013), www.cbo.gov/publication/43907.

Table 2-1.

CBO Projection of Operation and Support Costs in DoD's Base Budget, 2014 and 2018

(Billions of 2014 dollars)

	2014[a]	2018
Military Personnel		
Military personnel in the MHS	9	9
TRICARE for Life accrual payments	7	8
Other military personnel	125	126
Total, Appropriations for Military Personnel	**141**	**143**
Operation and Maintenance		
Civilian personnel		
Civilian personnel in the MHS	5	5
Other civilian personnel	62	62
Subtotal	67	67
Other O&M		
Other O&M in the MHS	28	31
Other O&M outside of the MHS[b]	120	120
Subtotal	148	152
Total, Appropriations for Operation and Maintenance	**215**	**218**
Total, Appropriations for Operation and Support	**356**	**361**
Memorandum:		
Military Health System		
Military personnel in the MHS	9	9
TRICARE for Life accrual payments	7	8
Civilian personnel in the MHS	5	5
Other O&M in the MHS	28	31
Total, Military Health System[c]	**49**	**54**
Compensation[d]		
Military personnel	141	143
Civilian personnel	67	67
Total, Compensation[e]	**208**	**210**

Source: Congressional Budget Office.

Notes: The CBO projection applies CBO's estimates of costs that are consistent with the Department of Defense's (DoD's) recent experience to DoD's plans.

      MHS = Military Health System; O&M = operation and maintenance.

a.   Costs for 2014 include $3.5 billion in the military personnel account and $2.1 billion in the O&M account that CBO shifted from the overseas contingency operations (OCO) budget into the base budget to fund 38,100 active-duty soldiers and marines. DoD plans to pay for those personnel with the OCO budget. Those positions will have been eliminated from the force by the end of 2017.

b.   For this analysis, CBO folded appropriations for most revolving funds (such as the one for the Defense Commissary Agency) into the appropriations for operation and maintenance. CBO treated as acquisition the accounts in the National Defense Sealift Fund that are used to purchase ships.

c.   These figures do not include MHS spending in accounts other than operation and support.

d.   Compensation consists of pay, cash benefits, and accrual payments for retirement benefits. For civilians, it also includes DoD's contributions for health insurance.

e.   These figures do not include compensation for civilian personnel funded from accounts other than operation and support.

Box 2-2.

The Context for the Projected Growth of Spending for Operation and Maintenance

To provide some context for projected spending for operation and maintenance (O&M), the Congressional Budget Office (CBO) calculated the historical O&M cost per active-duty service member and compared it to the future cost per active-duty service member implied by CBO's projection of the overall O&M budget. (O&M appropriations fund the day-to-day operations of the military, including, for example, equipment maintenance, training, civilian compensation, and most of the costs for military medical care.) CBO did not use that historical analysis to project the overall O&M budget, although it did use that approach to project the portion of O&M spending that does not reflect compensation for the Department of Defense's (DoD's) civilian employees or the cost of the military health system; rather, the future O&M cost per active-duty service member is an outcome of the planned end strength of the military forces and CBO's projection of the overall O&M budget.

From 1980 to 2001, the last year before the onset of major operations in Afghanistan and Iraq, DoD's average O&M cost per active-duty service member nearly doubled from $56,000 to $108,000 after adjusting for inflation (see the figure on the next page). Notably, the cost per active-duty service member grew by a roughly constant amount of about $2,300 a year—despite cyclical funding changes for DoD, including the military buildup of the 1980s and the reduction in forces at the end of the Cold War.

The overseas operations that began after 2001 caused rapid growth in O&M costs, which were funded largely through supplemental and emergency appropriations and not through the base budget. O&M funding per active-duty service member quickly departed from the historical trend as a result of the cost of conducting major operations on the other side of the world, the exceptional wear and tear on equipment in combat, and the large number of reserve and National Guard personnel deployed. (Because CBO's calculation involved dividing all O&M costs by the number of active-duty service members, deploying more reserve and National Guard personnel would tend to increase the O&M cost per active-duty service member in that calculation.) By 2010, O&M costs per active-duty service member had doubled again, reaching $221,000, including costs for overseas contingency operations.

The large growth in O&M spending to support operations in Afghanistan and Iraq obscures another significant trend that began in 2002—the rapid growth of O&M spending per active-duty service member in the base budget. That phenomenon is clearly illustrated in DoD's 2014 Future Years Defense Program: At $160,000 in 2014, the O&M cost in the base budget per active-duty service member is $27,000 (or about 20 percent) above what is implied by the trend between 1980 and 2001; that is, such spending has grown by an average of $4,000 per year since 2001, or about 75 percent faster than the historical rate. DoD expects that the O&M cost in the base budget per active-duty service member will fall slightly during the FYDP period, equaling $155,000 in 2018.

Continued

After 2018, according to CBO's projections, the ECI will continue to grow faster than the GDP deflator by 1.6 percentage points per year through 2028. (CBO used its published projection of the ECI through 2023 and extrapolated the ECI beyond that 10-year window by using the same annual growth rate for 2024 through 2028 that it projects for 2023.)

In enacting annual defense authorizations and appropriations, lawmakers often grant a raise in military pay that is greater than the one already specified in law. Ten of the last 13 annual pay raises were one-half of a percentage point greater than the rate of increase in the ECI, provided as part of ongoing efforts to eliminate a perceived "pay gap" between military compensation and compensation in the private sector. Whether such a gap existed and how to measure its magnitude have been

The Context for the Projected Growth of Spending for Operation and Maintenance

Costs of Operation and Maintenance per Active-Duty Service Member

(Thousands of 2014 dollars)

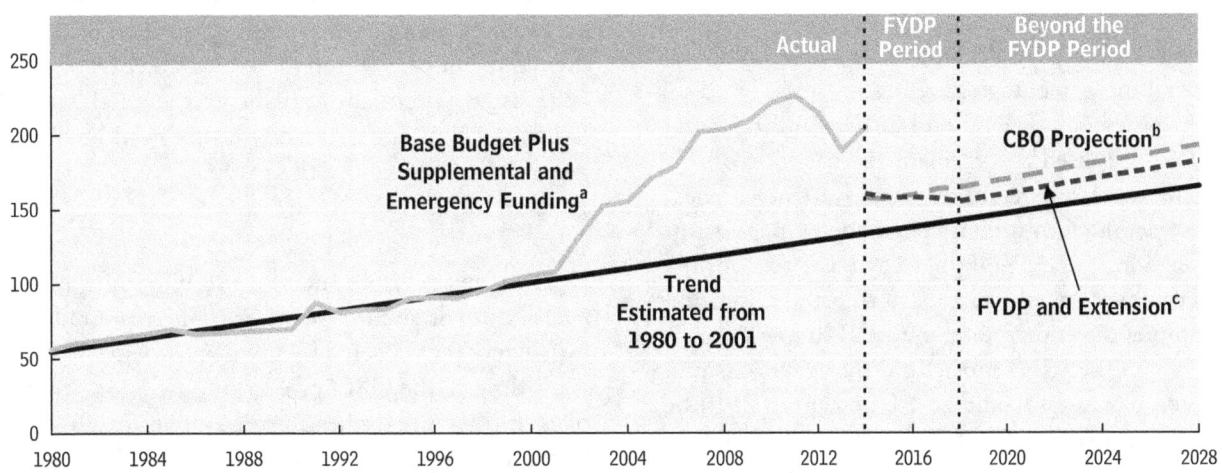

Source: Congressional Budget Office.

Note: DoD = Department of Defense; FYDP = Future Years Defense Program; OCO = overseas contingency operations;
         FYDP period = 2014 through 2018, the period for which DoD's plans are fully specified.

a.   No supplemental or emergency funding is shown for 2015 and later.

b.   The CBO projection of the base budget incorporates costs that are consistent with DoD's recent experience.

c.   For the extension of the FYDP, CBO projects the costs of DoD's plans using the department's estimates of costs to the extent they
      are available and costs that are consistent with CBO's projections of price and compensation trends in the overall economy when
      the department's estimates are not available.

The O&M cost per active-duty service member in the base budget grows at a faster rate in the CBO projection than in the FYDP, reaching $165,000 in 2018, reflecting an average annual increase of almost $2,000 from CBO's estimate of the 2014 cost. Beyond 2018, that cost in the CBO projection grows at an average annual rate of $2,800 a year, more than 20 percent faster than the $2,300 average annual growth rate from 1980 to 2001. Furthermore, growth in the CBO projection starts from a projected per capita cost in 2018 that is $22,000 higher than would have been predicted by the historical trend. In CBO's projection, the O&M cost exceeds $193,000 per active-duty service member by 2028.

matters of some debate.[6] The most recent three defense authorization acts (for fiscal years 2011, 2012, and 2013)

broke with previous practice and did not authorize a military pay raise in excess of the ECI.

DoD's plans in the 2014 FYDP go further, by proposing military pay raises that are smaller than CBO's projection of the corresponding rise in the ECI during the 2014–2018 period. The department's plans include a 1.0 percent pay raise each year for 2014 through 2016, and pay raises of 1.5 percent and 2.8 percent in 2017 and 2018, respectively. All of those raises are less than CBO's projected increases in the ECI. In its extension of the

---

6.   The most recent data indicate that military personnel are now earning more, on average, than over 80 percent of their civilian counterparts with equivalent education and years of experience. For a discussion of the adequacy of military pay in meeting recruiting, retention, and other goals, see Congressional Budget Office, *Costs of Military Pay and Benefits in the Defense Budget* (November 2012), www.cbo.gov/publication/43574.

FYDP, CBO assumed that military pay raises from 2019 through 2028 would equal the increases in the ECI. In the CBO projection, which is based on DoD's historical experience, CBO assumed that military pay increases would be 1.0 percent in 2014 (consistent with DoD's plans) but would keep pace with the growth in the ECI starting in 2015 and continuing through 2028.

DoD assumed that pay raises for its civilian employees would equal the percentage increases for military personnel for the years 2014, 2016, and 2017. For 2015 and 2018, DoD proposed that civilians receive raises of 0.5 percent and 1.5 percent, respectively, which are less than those planned for military personnel. CBO assumed in its extension of the FYDP that pay raises for DoD's civilian employees would keep pace with those for military personnel (and, therefore, the ECI) in every year after 2018.[7] In the CBO projection, the agency assumed that civilian pay raises would be 1.0 percent in 2014 but would equal growth in the ECI every year thereafter.

The Military Health System

Almost 10 million people are eligible for health care through DoD's TRICARE program. Eligible beneficiaries as of 2012 included 1.8 million military personnel from the active components or activated members of the reserves or National Guard, 2.6 million family members of those personnel, and 5.2 million military retirees and their family members. Beneficiaries may seek free or subsidized care from military treatment facilities, regional networks of civilian providers under contract with TRICARE, or other civilian providers. DoD also manages TRICARE for Life, a program that the Congress authorized in the 2001 National Defense Authorization Act to supplement Medicare for beneficiaries eligible for both Medicare and the military health benefit.

This report does not consider the costs of the benefits provided to veterans by the Department of Veterans Affairs (VA)—some $153 billion in that department's

2014 budget request. Those costs include $58 billion to provide health care to veterans who have service-connected disabilities or who meet certain other eligibility criteria. Other VA benefits include monthly cash payments that compensate for service-connected disabilities and GI Bill benefits that reimburse some of the costs of higher education. While TRICARE benefits are available to all of the roughly 2 million retired service members, most of whom served for 20 years or more, VA benefits are potentially available to the much larger population of 23 million veterans who received honorable or general discharges from their (typically shorter) military service.

DoD's plans for 2014 include $48 billion for military health care, or about 9 percent of the requested budget for all activities covered by the department's base budget. According to the CBO projection, the costs of DoD's plans for its military health care system for 2014 would be slightly higher, about $49 billion. CBO projects that such costs would reach $54 billion by 2018 and $70 billion by 2028 (see Figure 2-2). While the FYDP indicates that health care costs will grow at an average annual rate of 1.6 percent from 2014 to 2018, CBO projects a growth rate of 2.4 percent over the same period. Over the entire projection period from 2014 to 2028, CBO estimates an average growth rate of 2.6 percent per year. Those estimates are significantly lower than CBO projected in last year's version of this report primarily because of an economywide slowdown in health care spending and some technical revisions that CBO made in its estimating methods.

The CBO projection of DoD's medical costs consists of five categories:

■ *Military Personnel* covers pay and benefits for uniformed personnel assigned to work in the military health system. Those costs were included in the military personnel totals for pay, cash benefits, and retirement benefits (see Table 2-1 on page 21). They are included here as well because they contribute to the total cost of the military health system, but those costs are counted only once in CBO's projection of the entire base budget.[8]

---

7. CBO compared the annual pay raises of the two groups between 1984 and 2012. For the military pay raises, CBO included across-the-board pay raises as well as the average increases in years in which pay raises contained additional amounts targeted toward particular grades or seniority levels. For the civilian pay raises, CBO included across-the-board pay raises as well as the average increases in locality pay. Over those 29 years, the military pay raises were larger in 11 instances, the civil service pay raises were larger in 2 instances, and the raises were equal in the remaining 16 instances.

8. For example, the same $9 billion of funding for military personnel in the Military Health System in 2014 appears twice in Table 2-1, once in the accounting of the military personnel appropriation, and again in the total for the Military Health System.

Figure 2-2.

Costs of DoD's Plans for Its Military Health System

(Billions of 2014 dollars)

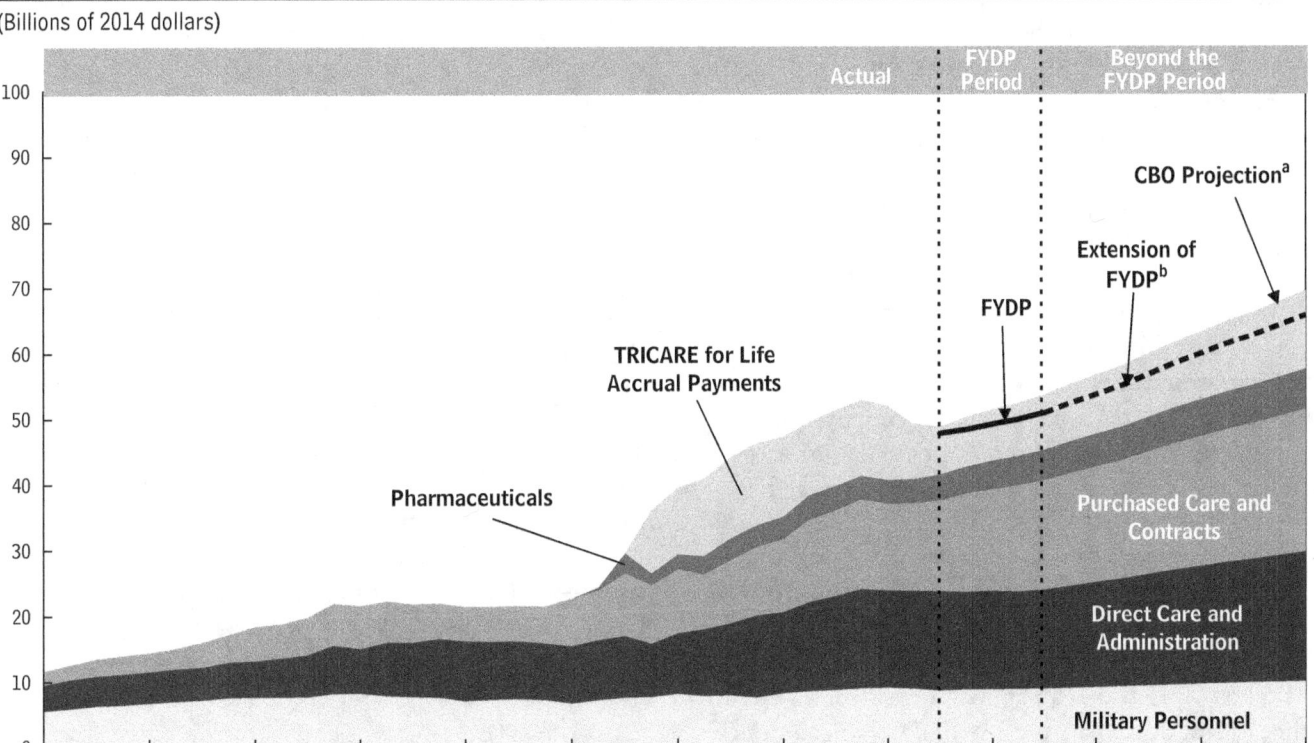

Source: Congressional Budget Office.

Notes: Supplemental and emergency funding for overseas contingency operations, such as those in Afghanistan and Iraq, is included for
2013 and earlier but not for later years.

Before 2001, pharmaceutical costs were not separately identifiable but were embedded in the costs of two categories: "Purchased
Care and Contracts" and "Direct Care and Administration." In 2001 and later years, most pharmaceutical costs are separately
identifiable, but some of those costs are embedded in the category "TRICARE for Life Accrual Payments."

The amounts shown for the Future Years Defense Program (FYDP) and the extension of the FYDP are the totals for all categories.

DoD = Department of Defense; FYDP period = 2014 through 2018, the period for which DoD's plans are fully specified.

a.   Each category shows the CBO projection of the base budget from 2014 to 2028. That projection incorporates costs that are consistent
with DoD's recent experience.

b.   For the extension of the FYDP (2019 to 2028), CBO projects the costs of DoD's plans using the department's estimates of costs to the
extent they are available and costs that are consistent with CBO's projections of price and compensation trends in the overall economy
when the department's estimates are not available.

- *Direct Care and Administration* covers the operation of
military medical facilities and other administrative
and training activities. This category includes pay and
benefits for civilian personnel assigned to work in
those facilities but excludes pay and benefits for
military personnel who work there.

- *Purchased Care and Contracts* covers medical care
delivered to military beneficiaries by providers in the
private sector, both inside and outside of the
TRICARE network.

- *Pharmaceuticals* covers purchases of medicines
dispensed at military medical facilities, at pharmacies
inside and outside of DoD's network, and through
DoD's mail-order pharmacy program.

- *Accrual Payments for TRICARE for Life* covers funds
deducted from DoD's discretionary budget
appropriation and credited to the Medicare-Eligible
Retiree Health Care Fund. Outlays from that fund are
used to reimburse military medical facilities for care
provided to military retirees and their family members

who are also eligible for Medicare and to cover most of the out-of-pocket costs that those beneficiaries would otherwise incur when seeking care from private-sector Medicare providers. (Those accrual charges were also included in the military personnel totals for pay, cash benefits, and retirement benefits, but are counted only once in CBO's projection of the entire base budget.)

CBO projects that pay and benefits for military personnel who work in the military health system will increase at the same rate as that for other military personnel. Those costs rise faster in the CBO projection than in DoD's FYDP because CBO assumed that, beginning in 2015, lawmakers would approve pay raises that kept up with the employment cost index. Nonetheless, military compensation is not a major contributor to the overall increase in costs that CBO projects for the military health system.

CBO estimated the costs of direct care and administration, purchased care and contracts, and pharmaceuticals between 2014 and 2018 using information from DoD's FYDP but made two adjustments that raised estimated costs. First, CBO added an annual increase of 1 percent to the costs of direct care because DoD's projection that such costs will be unchanged in real terms over the FYDP period is not consistent with historical experience. Also, CBO added the Administration's estimates of savings in purchased care and pharmacy costs that would result from beneficiary cost-sharing initiatives that DoD has requested and that the Congress has regularly prevented from taking effect.

CBO assumed that, after 2018, the per capita costs of military health care would grow at the same rates that CBO projects for health care nationwide apart from the Medicare program (because the latter program differs in important ways from the rest of the nation's health care system).[9] Over the entire 2014–2028 period in the CBO projection, the real annual growth rates of cost per user in the military health system average 1.9 percent for direct care and administration, 3.3 percent for purchased care and contracts, and 3.0 percent for pharmaceuticals.[10]

Out-of-pocket costs borne by TRICARE beneficiaries have increased much more slowly than nationwide health care costs. DoD estimated that in 2012, a typical military retiree could enroll his or her family in TRICARE Prime (the TRICARE option most similar to a health maintenance organization, or HMO) for $520 per year and would, on average, pay another $445 in copayments and other fees for a total annual cost of $965. In contrast, DoD estimated that a civilian in the general U.S. population who enrolled in a family HMO plan offered by an employer would typically pay $5,080 as the employee's share of annual premiums. With deductibles and copayments averaging $1,000, that family would pay a total of $6,080 over the course of the year. Thus, the family enrolled in TRICARE Prime would pay costs that are 16 percent of what a similar family would pay for coverage in a civilian HMO. On the basis of a parallel calculation, DoD estimated that a family who used TRICARE Standard (which operates as a traditional fee-for-service plan) or Extra (which operates as a preferred-provider organization, or PPO) would pay 19 percent of what a similar family would pay for coverage in a civilian PPO.[11]

As a result of those cost differences, a growing share of military retirees and their dependents are relying on TRICARE rather than participating in health insurance provided by civilian employers or purchasing insurance on their own.[12] In addition, low out-of-pocket costs and other factors have led to usage rates for inpatient and outpatient care that DoD has found to be higher for TRICARE Prime enrollees than for comparable civilians enrolled in HMOs.[13]

In order to reduce the rate of growth of its health care costs, DoD's 2014 budget request would implement the

---

9. See Congressional Budget Office, *The 2013 Long-Term Budget Outlook* (September 2013), p. 38, www.cbo.gov/publication/ 44521. CBO's estimates using this approach are very similar to those that would result from applying DoD-specific excess growth factors to the National Health Expenditure (NHE) projections developed by the Centers for Medicare & Medicaid Services. See *National Health Expenditure Projections, 2011–2021,* http://go.usa.gov/WD9V.

10. In nominal terms, those average annual growth rates for the 2014–2028 period would be 4.0 percent for direct care and administration, 5.4 percent for purchased care and contracts, and 5.1 percent for pharmaceuticals. The calculation of the growth rate for pharmaceuticals excludes some pharmacy costs that are not paid explicitly from O&M funds but are embedded in the accrual payments for TRICARE for Life.

11. Department of Defense, *Evaluation of the TRICARE Program— Access, Cost and Quality: Fiscal Year 2013 Report to Congress* (February 2013), pp. 83 and 85, http://go.usa.gov/jX9H.

12. In 2001, about 50 percent of military retirees and their dependents had signed up for private health insurance, but by 2012 that figure had dropped to 23 percent. Ibid., p. 82.

13. Ibid., pp. 67 and 72.

following changes to the TRICARE benefit beginning in that year:

- Institute an annual fee for military retirees who are newly eligible for Medicare and enroll in TRICARE for Life;

- Increase the annual fee that military retirees who are not yet eligible for Medicare pay to enroll in TRICARE Prime;

- Institute an annual fee for military retirees who are not yet eligible for Medicare and enroll in TRICARE Standard or Extra;

- Increase the annual deductibles for military retirees who are not yet eligible for Medicare and enroll in TRICARE Standard or Extra; and

- Adjust the pharmacy copayments for active-duty family members and for retirees and their families as a further incentive to purchase mail-order and generic drugs.[14]

DoD estimates that those changes would generate savings of $4.5 billion in the department's O&M account and $4.7 billion in accrual payments into the Medicare-Eligible Retiree Health Care Fund over the next five years. Those savings are incorporated into DoD's projections of the funding it will seek through 2018. Because the Congress has a long history of denying DoD's requests to increase cost sharing by TRICARE beneficiaries, the CBO projection incorporates the assumption that the savings generated by DoD's proposed fee increases starting in 2014 would not be realized. Indeed, the House of Representatives' version of the National Defense Authorization Act for 2014 (H.R.1960) would reject those DoD proposals; the full Senate has not yet voted on its version of the National Defense Authorization Act, but the bill passed by committee would also reject those DoD proposals.

In the CBO projection, DoD's accrual payments for TRICARE for Life would grow at an average annual rate per service member of 3.6 percent (after adjusting for inflation) between 2014 and 2028. That projection is derived from the DoD Office of the Actuary's projection that annual accrual payments per service member will rise

at a nominal rate of 5.75 percent for the foreseeable future.

The costs of the military health system in the CBO projection exceed those in the extension of the FYDP. The annual growth rates are somewhat higher in the CBO projection than in the FYDP itself through 2018. For 2019 and beyond, costs begin and remain at a higher level in the CBO projection, although the growth rates in the two projections are the same through 2028. CBO's current projections of military health care spending in the 2020s are below CBO's projections based on the 2013 FYDP for three reasons.[15] First, growth in health care costs in the United States has slowed in recent years. Second, the amount by which growth in DoD's health care spending has exceeded growth in national health care spending has diminished, reflecting some success by DoD in slowing growth in its health care costs, particularly for pharmaceuticals. Finally, CBO made some technical revisions to its projections that resulted in lower estimates.

Other Operation and Maintenance Costs

The remainder of O&S spending is for "other O&M"— the portions of operation and maintenance other than compensation for military personnel and DoD's civilian employees and the military health system. CBO also includes appropriations for most revolving funds in the other O&M category. Per active-duty service member, other O&M costs have grown steadily since 1980.

In DoD's 2014 FYDP, other O&M costs would fall from $118 billion in 2014 to $114 billion in 2015 and remain at about that amount through 2018. Costs would fall, in part, to meet targets for budget reduction that the Office of Management and Budget (OMB) has specified for 2017 through 2021.[16] However, neither OMB nor DoD has provided details as to how those targets would be achieved. In contrast, under the CBO projection, other O&M costs would be $120 billion in 2014 and then decline to $116 billion in 2015 before gradually

---

14. Department of Defense, *Fiscal Year 2014 Budget Request: Overview* (April 2013), pp. 5-3–5-6, http://go.usa.gov/WDNm.

15. Congressional Budget Office, *Long-Term Implications of the 2013 Future Years Defense Program* (July 2012), www.cbo.gov/publication/43428.

16. Office of Management and Budget, *OMB Sequestration Preview Report to the President and Congress for Fiscal Year 2014 and OMB Report to the Congress on the Joint Committee Reductions for Fiscal Year 2014* (corrected version May 20, 2013), Table 1, p. 4, www.whitehouse.gov/omb/legislative_reports/sequestration.

increasing to $120 billion again in 2018. In 2014, costs under the CBO projection are higher than DoD's request because it includes in the base budget all of the O&M costs associated with active-duty personnel, including those that DoD proposes to pay from its OCO budget. In addition, because the FYDP does not specify how DoD will meet OMB's proposed budget reductions, CBO removed those reductions from its projection.

For costs beyond the FYDP period, CBO used the same method to project other O&M costs under the CBO projection and under the extension of the FYDP. Because a diverse array of functions contribute to the remaining O&M costs, it was not practical for CBO to build an estimate beyond the FYDP period from the "bottom up"—that is, developing estimates for the costs of the various components involved and summing those estimates—as CBO does for the projections of the costs of compensation and military health care. Instead, CBO used a "top-down" approach to project other O&M costs for the years beyond the FYDP. Specifically, CBO used historical growth in other O&M costs per active-duty service member (about $1,100 per year in 2014 dollars from 1980 to 2001) to project costs from 2019 to 2028 in both the CBO projection and the extension of the FYDP. The source of that historical growth cannot be readily determined from the aggregate data; it could have been caused by a number of factors. For example, new weapon systems tend to be more costly to operate because they are more complex and technically sophisticated than are earlier generations of weapons. In addition, aging weapon systems tend to be more costly to operate and maintain, particularly as they approach the end of their service life or as they are upgraded to extend their service life. Finally, DoD may have increased its hiring of contractors over time to provide services and functions that did not exist in earlier years or that had previously been provided by military personnel.

Projections of Acquisition Costs

Acquisition funding is used to develop and purchase weapon systems and other major equipment and to upgrade the capabilities or extend the service life of weapon systems. Such funding is the sum of the appropriations for procurement and for research, development, test, and evaluation.[1] For 2014, the Administration requested $167 billion for acquisition—32 percent of its total request for the Department of Defense excluding funding for overseas contingency operations.

Under the Congressional Budget Office projection, the costs to implement DoD's plans for acquisition over the next five years would rise steadily to $189 billion (in 2014 dollars) in 2018; that amount would be 13 percent above the amount in 2014 (see Figure 3-1). In 2019, the first year beyond the period covered by the Future Years Defense Program, the costs of DoD's acquisition plans would increase sharply, by 6 percent, to $201 billion. Costs would remain at about that level through 2025 but would decrease thereafter, dipping to $181 billion (in 2014 dollars) by 2028.

The steep increase in acquisition costs beyond the FYDP suggests that a classic "bow wave" is being created by DoD's constraining acquisition during a period of tight budgets but continuing to plan for more acquisition thereafter (for example, in the Navy's 30-year shipbuilding plan). Bow waves beyond the FYDP period had been a common feature of DoD's plans for many years, particularly during periods of flat or declining budgets. For most of the last decade, however, bow waves largely disappeared because budgets grew steadily and there was an expectation by DoD that steady growth would continue. With the Budget Control Act of 2011 restraining the growth of appropriations, especially in the near term, a substantial bow wave has reemerged. The BCA may also explain another aspect of the services' plans for acquisition: lower costs in 2013 and 2014 than in 2012 or 2015.

Because acquisition can be easier to cut quickly than activities funded through other accounts, such as military personnel, DoD appears to have disproportionately used cuts to acquisition to accommodate the limits on funding imposed by the BCA.

Under DoD's estimates for the FYDP, acquisition costs would increase 5 percent to $176 billion in 2015 but then remain roughly constant between 2015 and 2018, averaging $174 billion over that period. In its extension of the FYDP, CBO estimates that acquisition costs would increase by another 5 percent from 2018 to 2019 and remain at that higher level—an average of $182 billion per year—through 2025 before decreasing through 2028. From 2019 to 2028, total costs would be 9 percent lower under the extension of the FYDP than under the CBO projection, primarily because of differences in estimates of the costs of new weapon systems. Specifically, costs for weapon systems that are not yet in full production are typically higher under the CBO projection than under the extension of the FYDP, reflecting CBO's higher estimates that are based on DoD's historical experience with the costs of developing weapons systems.[2]

DoD has requested additional acquisition funding to continue supporting the overseas contingency operations in Afghanistan and elsewhere. For 2001 to 2013, more than $330 billion in OCO funds was appropriated for acquisition. Those funds have been used for a variety of purposes, including replacing equipment destroyed in

---

1. CBO also includes as acquisition portions of the National Defense Sealift Fund used to develop or purchase sealift ships.

2. Historical analysis of DoD's acquisition programs indicates that costs have grown substantially relative to initial estimates. See Mark V. Arena and others, *Historical Cost Growth of Completed Weapon System Programs,* TR343-AF (prepared by the RAND Corporation for the United States Air Force, 2006), http://tinyurl.com/nay4kvb; and Obaid Younossi and others, *Is Weapon System Cost Growth Increasing? A Quantitative Assessment of Completed and Ongoing Programs,* MG-588-AF (prepared by the RAND Corporation for the United States Air Force, 2007), http://tinyurl.com/o4uj3nt.

Figure 3-1.

Costs of DoD's Acquisition Plans

(Billions of 2014 dollars)

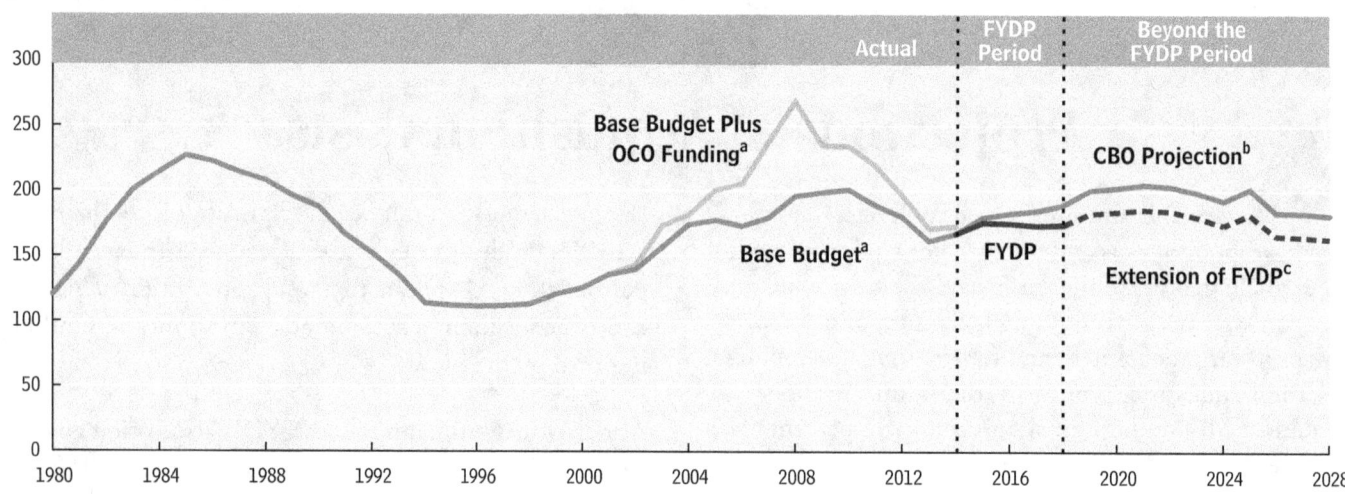

Source: Congressional Budget Office.

Note: DoD = Department of Defense; FYDP = Future Years Defense Program; OCO = overseas contingency operations; FYDP period = 2014 through 2018, the period for which DoD's plans are fully specified.

a.   Base-budget data include supplemental and emergency funding before 2002. For 2002 to 2014, supplemental and emergency funding for overseas contingency operations, such as those in Afghanistan and Iraq, and for other purposes is shown separately from the base-budget data. No OCO funding is shown for 2015 and later.

b.   The CBO projection of the base budget incorporates costs that are consistent with DoD's recent experience.

c.   For the extension of the FYDP (2019 to 2028), CBO projects the costs of DoD's plans using the department's estimates of costs to the extent they are available and costs that are consistent with CBO's projections of price and compensation trends in the overall economy when the department's estimates are not available.

battle and purchasing new types of equipment, such as mine-resistant vehicles. For 2014, $5.7 billion of the $79 billion requested for overseas operations is for acquisition: $5.6 billion is for procurement and $72 million is for RDT&E. This report does not address those costs.

To project the costs of DoD's acquisition plans, CBO tracked the procurement and RDT&E funding for more than 190 weapon systems or major upgrades to existing systems. Some of those systems are in or nearing production (for example, the Air Force's KC-46 tanker), and some are in the early planning stages (for example, the new ground combat vehicle planned for the Army). Others (for instance, a replacement for the Navy's F/A-18E/F fighter) have no specific plans yet but have been identified by CBO either as systems that would be necessary to maintain weapon inventories when existing systems reach the end of their service life and need to be replaced, or as systems that would provide new capabilities to meet the goals described in the services' policy statements.

The following sections describe details of the most significant systems in DoD's acquisition plans and CBO's estimates of the costs of those plans for each of the military departments—the Army, the Navy (which also includes the Marine Corps), and the Air Force—and for the parts of DoD outside of the military services, including the Missile Defense Agency (MDA) (see Figure 3-2).

The Army

The Department of the Army's 2014 request for acquisition funding includes $24 billion for the base budget plus an additional $2.7 billion for overseas contingency operations. According to the CBO projection of DoD's plans, acquisition costs for the Army's base budget would increase to $27 billion in 2015 (an increase of 14 percent) and remain at about that level through the end of the FYDP period (see Figure 3-3). In 2019 (the first year after the FYDP period), costs would rise sharply to about $35 billion and then would decline gradually through

Figure 3-2.

Costs of DoD's Acquisition Plans, by Military Service

(Billions of 2014 dollars)

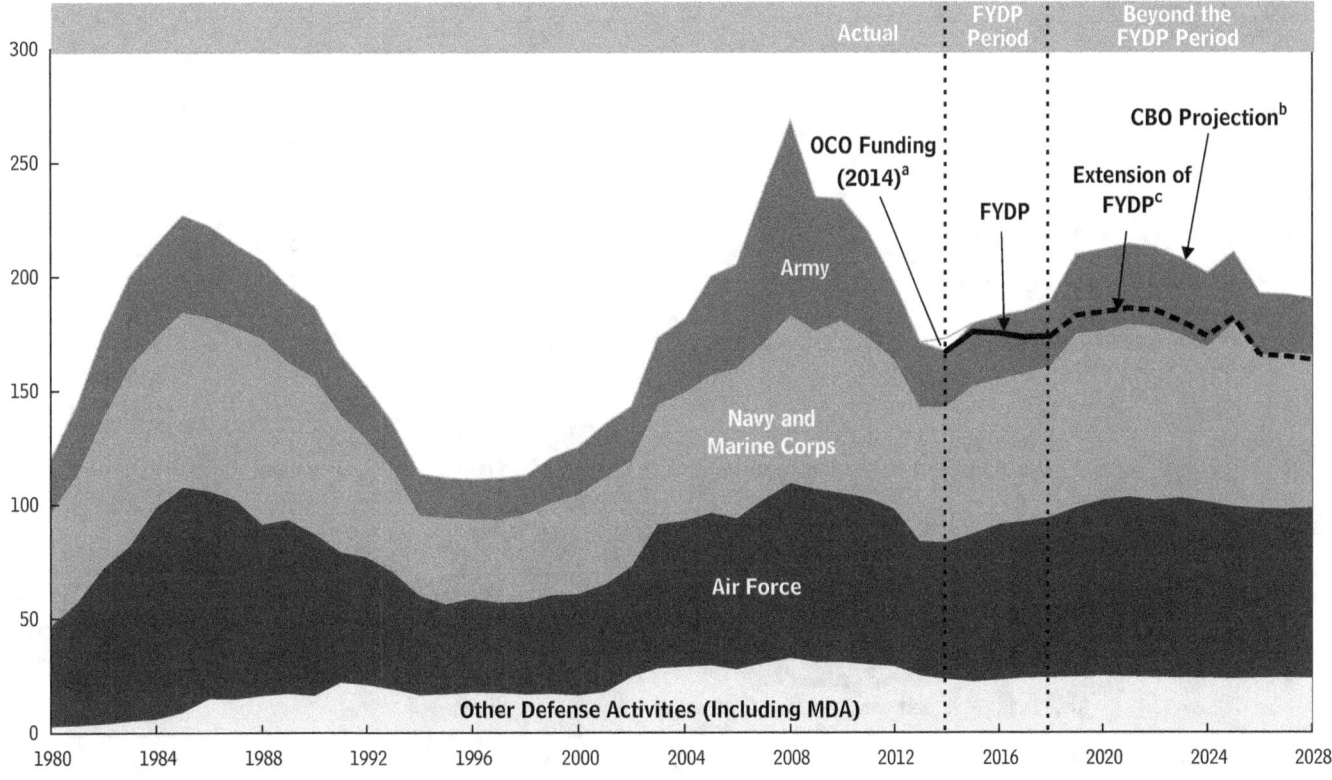

Source: Congressional Budget Office.

Notes: The amounts shown for the Future Years Defense Program (FYDP) and the extension of the FYDP are the totals for all categories.

DoD = Department of Defense; OCO = overseas contingency operations; FYDP period = 2014 through 2018, the period for which DoD's plans are fully specified; MDA = Missile Defense Agency.

a. Supplemental and emergency funding for overseas contingency operations, such as those in Afghanistan and Iraq, is included in the individual categories for 2013 and earlier; it is shown separately for 2014 and is not included for later years.

b. Each category shows the CBO projection of the base budget from 2014 to 2028. That projection incorporates costs that are consistent with DoD's recent experience.

c. For the extension of the FYDP (2019 to 2028), CBO projects the costs of DoD's plans using the department's estimates of costs to the extent they are available and costs that are consistent with CBO's projections of price and compensation trends in the overall economy when the department's estimates are not available.

2025 before dropping more noticeably thereafter. The higher estimated costs between 2019 and 2025 would result primarily from purchases of ground combat vehicles and trucks. The extension of the FYDP has a similar profile, but its total estimated costs for 2019 through 2028 are 18 percent lower than the costs estimated in the CBO projection.

For its projections of procurement costs for the Army, CBO tracked selected programs in five categories of major systems: ground combat vehicles and trucks; command, control, communications, computers,

intelligence, surveillance, and reconnaissance (C4ISR) systems; aircraft; missile defense systems; and missiles and munitions. The remaining programs are grouped together as "other procurement."[3] Funding for RDT&E is displayed as a separate category.

---

3. CBO's procurement categories do not directly correspond with service appropriation accounts. For example, CBO's category for Army aircraft includes only major programs contained in the broader "Aircraft Procurement, Army" appropriation account. Smaller programs in that account are included in CBO's other procurement category.

Figure 3-3.

Costs of the Army's Acquisition Plans

(Billions of 2014 dollars)

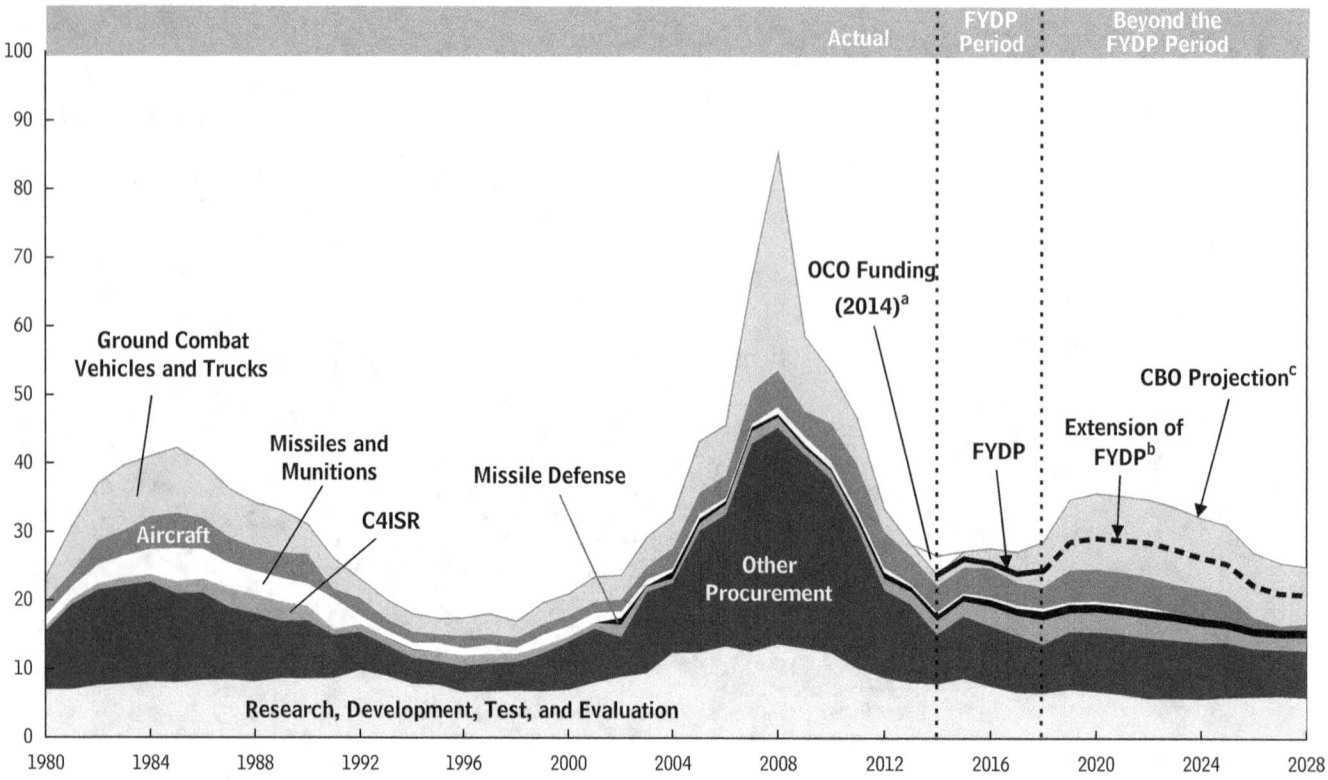

Source: Congressional Budget Office.

Notes: The amounts shown for the Future Years Defense Program (FYDP) and the extension of the FYDP are the totals for all categories.

OCO = overseas contingency operations; FYDP period = 2014 through 2018, the period for which the Department of Defense's (DoD's) plans are fully specified; C4ISR = command, control, communications, computers, intelligence, surveillance, and reconnaissance.

a.   Supplemental and emergency funding for overseas contingency operations, such as those in Afghanistan and Iraq, is included in the individual categories for 2013 and earlier; it is shown separately for 2014 and is not included for later years.

b.   For the extension of the FYDP (2019 to 2028), CBO projects the costs of DoD's plans using the department's estimates of costs to the extent they are available and costs that are consistent with CBO's projections of price and compensation trends in the overall economy when the department's estimates are not available.

c.   Each category shows the CBO projection of the base budget from 2014 to 2028. That projection incorporates costs that are consistent with DoD's recent experience.

Ground Combat Vehicles and Trucks

The Army's plans include upgrades to some of its combat vehicles, including Abrams tanks, Bradley fighting vehicles, and self-propelled 155-millimeter howitzers. The plans also include the purchase of two new types of combat vehicles, the ground combat vehicle (GCV) and the armored multipurpose vehicle (AMPV). The Army intends to use the GCV, which would be an entirely new vehicle, to replace the infantry carrier version of the Bradley fighting vehicle in its combat brigades.[4] The AMPV,

which is based on existing vehicles, would replace the various versions of the M113 armored personnel carrier in the Army's combat brigades. Procurement funding for the new GCVs would begin in 2018, and purchases would exceed 100 vehicles per year by 2020. Purchases of AMPVs would also begin in 2018.

---

4.   For a detailed analysis of the GCV, see Congressional Budget Office, *The Army's Ground Combat Vehicle Program and Alternatives* (April 2013), www.cbo.gov/publication/44044.

In addition, the Army intends to modernize or upgrade some of its tactical vehicles, which are primarily various types of trucks. The Army's plans include the purchase of a light truck that is being developed in cooperation with the Marine Corps and is expected to be better protected and more fuel-efficient than the Army's current light truck, the high-mobility multipurpose wheeled vehicle (HMMWV). During the next 15 years, the Army plans to purchase about 25,000 of those new trucks. The Army ultimately plans to replace about one-third of the roughly 150,000 HMMWVs in its inventory with that new vehicle. The Army also has plans to extend the service life of its heavy and medium trucks.

C4ISR Systems

The Army's C4ISR systems include radios and other equipment that enable Army units to communicate and share data. Two of the larger programs in this category are for new advanced radios, the Joint Tactical Radio System (JTRS) and the Warfighter Information Network (WIN-T) data-networking system. The Army is scheduled to buy almost 230,000 radios through the JTRS program from 2014 through 2028; it plans to purchase hardware and software through the WIN-T program in three increments through 2028 to provide increasingly sophisticated networking capabilities.

Aircraft

The Army's plans for aviation programs include both manned and unmanned aircraft. Those plans include completing purchases of UH-72A Lakota light-utility helicopters, which are replacing the remaining UH-1H Hueys and OH-58C Kiowas. The Army is also exploring options for procuring Armed Scout Helicopters to replace today's fleet of OH-58D Kiowa Warriors and the canceled Armed Reconnaissance Helicopter. In both of its projections, CBO assumed that procurement of the new helicopter would begin in 2018. The projections for Army aircraft also include development of a future vertical lift aircraft, production of which would not begin in earnest until after 2028. In addition, the projections include the Army's plans to upgrade and extend the service life of its Apache, Blackhawk, and Chinook helicopters. The projections also include plans to purchase several types of unmanned aircraft, including the MQ-1C Grey Eagle, which is similar to the Predator aircraft flown by the Air Force.[5]

Missile Defense

The Army's plans include purchases of equipment to defend against ballistic missiles. In recent years, the Army had planned to buy two systems: the Patriot Air and Missile Defense System, which includes the Patriot Advanced Capability-3 (PAC-3) missile, and the Patriot/Medium Extended Air Defense System (MEADS) Combined Aggregate Program, which was intended to be a follow-on to the Patriot system. However, in February 2011, DoD announced that the Army would not purchase MEADS but instead would terminate the program after a limited development effort, and no funds were requested for MEADS in 2014. Current plans continue to include procurement of the Patriot Missile Segment Enhancement interceptor, which is compatible with Patriot and MEADS and is expected to perform better than the PAC-3 missile, in quantities similar to those anticipated in the MEADS program before it was terminated. The Army now plans to upgrade other components of the existing Patriot systems as well.

The Navy and the Marine Corps

The 2014 budget request contains $60 billion for acquisition in the base budget for the Department of the Navy, which includes the Navy and the Marine Corps, and an additional $694 million for acquisition for overseas contingency operations. According to the CBO projection of DoD's plans, acquisition costs for the Navy and the Marine Corps would rise to $66 billion in 2018—an increase of 10 percent. Acquisition costs would average $64 billion from 2014 through 2018, 3 percent higher than the average anticipated in the FYDP (see Figure 3-4).

Beyond the FYDP period, according to CBO's projection, the costs to implement the Navy and Marine Corps' acquisition plans would increase substantially, jumping to $76 billion in 2019 (or by 16 percent over the 2018 amount) and remain above $70 billion per year through 2023. Except for a spike in ship procurement in 2025, costs would then decline to $67 billion in 2028. The FYDP and its extension have a similar profile, but the total estimated costs for 2019 through 2028 are 7 percent lower than the costs estimated in the CBO projection.

---

5. For related discussion, see Congressional Budget Office, *Policy Options for Unmanned Aircraft Systems* (June 2011), www.cbo.gov/publication/41448.

Figure 3-4.

Costs of the Navy and Marine Corps' Acquisition Plans

(Billions of 2014 dollars)

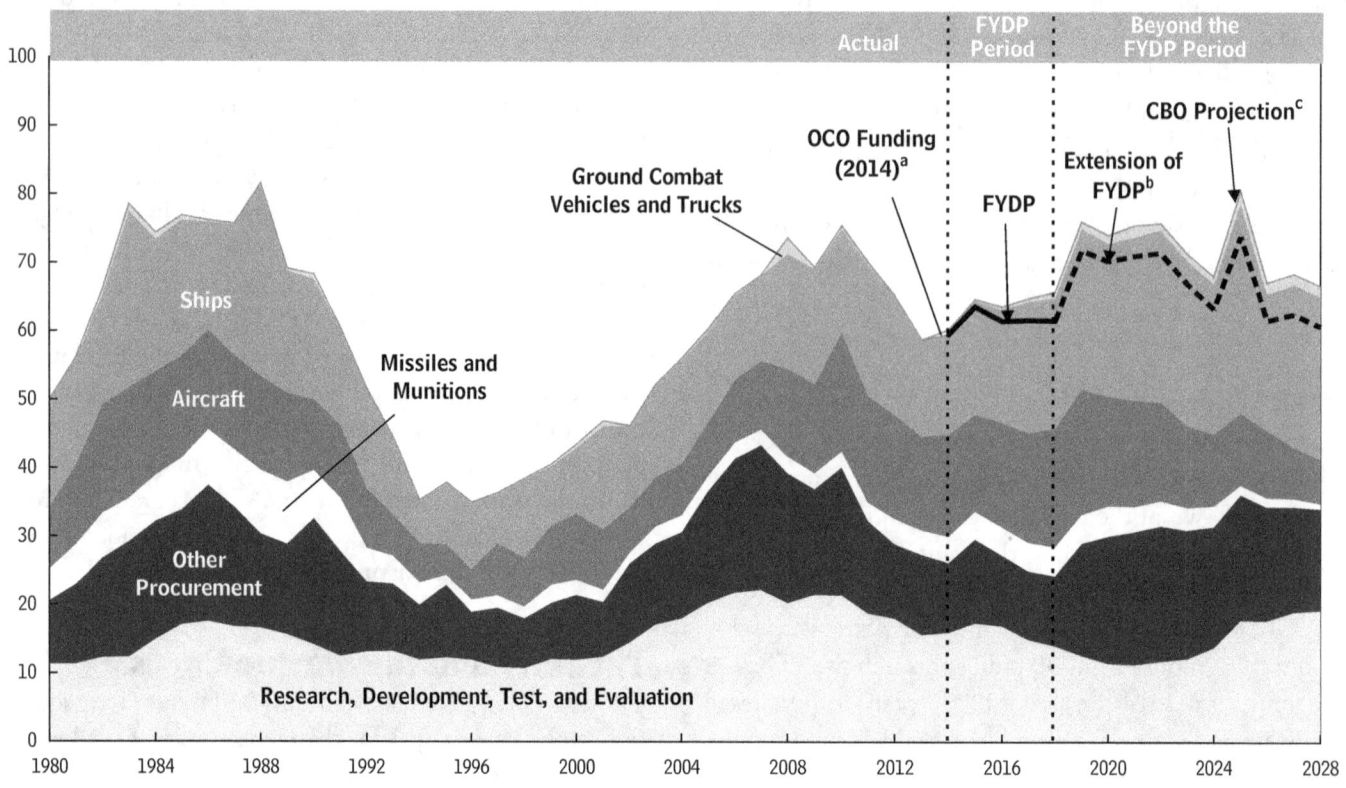

Source: Congressional Budget Office.

Notes: The amounts shown for the Future Years Defense Program (FYDP) and the extension of the FYDP are the totals for all categories.

OCO = overseas contingency operations; FYDP period = 2014 through 2018, the period for which the Department of Defense's (DoD's) plans are fully specified.

a. Supplemental and emergency funding for overseas contingency operations, such as those in Afghanistan and Iraq, is included in the individual categories for 2013 and earlier; it is shown separately for 2014 and is not included for later years.

b. For the extension of the FYDP (2019 to 2028), CBO projects the costs of DoD's plans using the department's estimates of costs to the extent they are available and costs that are consistent with CBO's projections of price and compensation trends in the overall economy when the department's estimates are not available.

c. Each category shows the CBO projection of the base budget from 2014 to 2028. That projection incorporates costs that are consistent with DoD's recent experience.

In analyzing procurement costs for the Navy and the Marine Corps, CBO tracked selected programs in four categories of major systems: ships, aircraft, ground combat vehicles (trucks and armored vehicles for the Marine Corps), and missiles and munitions. The remaining procurement programs are grouped together as other procurement. As with the Army, funding for RDT&E is shown separately.

Ships

The Navy requested $14.5 billion in 2014 for programs that fall into CBO's ship category. Included in that total are $13.6 billion for ship construction and major modifications plus additional funding for ships purchased through the National Defense Sealift Fund and for mission modules purchased for littoral combat ships (LCSs). The Navy's current plans reflect the goal of expanding the fleet from today's 286 ships to 306 ships. According to the CBO projection, those plans would cost an average of

$22 billion per year between 2014 and 2028. Costs for 2014 through 2028 would average $0.9 billion per year more under the CBO projection than under the FYDP and its extension.[6]

Surface Combatants. The planned increase in the Navy's fleet is primarily in the surface combatant force, which currently consists of 105 cruisers, destroyers, frigates, and LCSs. By 2028, the surface combatant fleet would grow to 141 ships under the Navy's plans—including 51 LCSs, which are smaller and faster than any of today's other surface combatants.

The Navy's plans for the surface combatant force changed somewhat between the submissions of the 2013 and 2014 budgets. The Navy's new force structure assessment, released earlier this year, includes an inventory objective of 88 large surface combatants (cruisers and destroyers) compared with about 90 under last year's budget. The Navy now has 84 cruisers and destroyers in the fleet but will retire 7 cruisers early in 2015. (The Navy had planned to retire those cruisers as part of last year's budget, but Congress instructed the Navy to keep them in service and provided additional funding to do so. Such funding has not been provided to keep them in service beyond 2014, however.) The Navy is continuing with its plan to build new DDG-51 destroyers and intends to begin purchasing substantially upgraded DDG-51 destroyers in 2016; from 2014 through 2028, the Navy plans to buy 34 DDG-51s. The Navy's plans would allow the service to achieve an inventory objective of 88 large surface combatants in 2021 and between 2024 and 2028.

With respect to small surface combatants—frigates and LCSs—the Navy plans to build two versions of the LCS through at least 2015. It previously planned to select one of two competing designs but has opted to continue building both versions. The Navy's force structure assessment reduced the goal from 55 to 52 LCSs, and the service intends to complete the purchase of those ships by 2026.

Submarines. The Navy's plans would lead to a reduction in the submarine force from its current level. Although the Navy's stated goal is to have 48 attack submarines (SSNs) through the projection period, its plans for procurement would meet that goal through 2024 but then fall below that number thereafter. The Navy intends to replace the 14 ballistic missile submarines (SSBNs) of the Ohio class that are in service today with 12 new submarines starting in 2021. From 2026 through the end of the projection period, one SSBN would be purchased each year at an average cost of nearly $7 billion. According to the Navy's plans, none of the four guided-missile submarines (SSGNs) that are scheduled for retirement will be replaced.

Amphibious and Maritime Prepositioning Ships. The Navy's plans call for a force of 33 amphibious ships, including 11 large-deck amphibious assault ships. Under those plans, the Navy would purchase 3 amphibious assault ships through 2028. The projections also incorporate the Navy's plans to begin buying a replacement for the LSD-41 and LSD-49 dock landing ships in 2019, one year later than under the 2013 budget. That new ship is designated the LX(R); 6 of a planned 11 of those ships would be purchased by 2028.[7]

Aircraft Carriers. The Navy's plans include a future carrier force of 11 large-deck ships, all of which would be nuclear-powered. The Navy ordered the first of its new class of aircraft carriers, the USS *Gerald R. Ford* (CVN-78), in 2008. The Navy ordered the second ship of that class in 2013, and it plans to order another ship every five years thereafter. In addition, plans provide for the refueling and overhaul of 6 of today's Nimitz class carriers (including continued funding for the ongoing refueling and overhaul of the USS *Theodore Roosevelt*) over the projection period. The Navy expects to maintain a fleet of 11 aircraft carriers for all but three years of the projection period; the fleet would briefly drop to 10 aircraft carriers between 2013, when the USS *Enterprise* was retired, and 2016, when the USS *Gerald R. Ford* is expected to enter the fleet.

---

6. CBO's extension of the FYDP is, for Navy shipbuilding, based on the Navy's explicit 30-year shipbuilding plans and associated cost estimates. The CBO projection is based on the same plans but with CBO's estimates of costs. For more details, see Congressional Budget Office, *An Analysis of the Navy's Fiscal Year 2014 Shipbuilding Plan* (October 2013), www.cbo.gov/publication/44655.

---

7. For related analysis, see Congressional Budget Office, *An Analysis of the Navy's Amphibious Warfare Ships for Deploying Marines Overseas* (November 2011), www.cbo.gov/publication/42716.

Aircraft

The Department of the Navy's aviation programs include Navy and Marine Corps aircraft and aircraft-related weapon systems. For 2014, the Administration requested $14 billion to procure 165 new aircraft. According to the CBO projection, the Navy's plans for aircraft would cost an average of $13 billion per year between 2014 and 2028. Average annual funding would be considerably higher in the earlier years of the projection period—$15 billion annually over the next ten years—because of simultaneous purchases of several types of fixed- and rotary-wing aircraft; once the production of those aircraft was completed in 2022, average costs would drop below $13 billion. That decrease contributes to the drop in overall acquisition costs in the later years of the projection period. In the absence of future changes in the number of aircraft operated by the Navy and the Marine Corps, costs would be expected to increase again beyond the projection period as aircraft that are relatively new today would reach the end of their service lives and be replaced.

Fighter Aircraft. Plans for naval fighter aircraft call for completing procurement of EA-18G electronic warfare aircraft in 2014, continuing development of the F-35 Joint Strike Fighter (both the F-35B short takeoff/vertical landing version and the F-35C carrier-based version), and initiating development of a new fighter to replace F/A-18E/Fs that are expected to reach the end of their service lives after 2025. Both the CBO projection and the extension of the FYDP reflect CBO's assumption that the Navy will opt for a new fighter design to replace the F/A-18E/F. Projected costs for that new fighter within the projection period are primarily for research and development beginning in 2016; initial production is assumed to begin in 2027.[8]

Other Fixed-Wing Aircraft. In addition to fighters, the Navy plans to purchase several other types of carrier- and land-based fixed-wing aircraft, including a new version of the carrier-based E-2 Hawkeye airborne early-warning aircraft; a new land-based patrol aircraft, the P-8A Poseidon, which is based on a Boeing 737 airframe and is to replace the P-3C Orion; an unmanned maritime surveillance aircraft, the MQ-4 Triton, that is a modified version of the Air Force's Global Hawk high-altitude unmanned aerial vehicle; and carrier-based unmanned combat air vehicles capable of conducting surveillance, reconnaissance, or strike missions.[9]

Tilt-Rotor and Rotary-Wing Aircraft. The Navy's plans include purchases of MH-60R/S helicopters and MQ-8A Firescout unmanned helicopters. The Navy is also evaluating options for a VXX aircraft to replace the current Marine One Presidential transport helicopters. CBO's analysis reflects the assumption that the new program would begin delivering replacements for Marine One in the second half of this decade.

The Marine Corps' plans also call for completing the replacement or upgrade of nearly every component of its tilt-rotor and rotary-wing forces. The Marine Corps is replacing its CH-46E medium-lift helicopters with MV-22 Osprey tilt-rotor aircraft and is modernizing its fleets of UH-1N light-utility helicopters and AH-1W attack helicopters with a mix of new and remanufactured aircraft. In addition, the Marine Corps is proceeding with plans to modernize its fleet of heavy-lift CH-53E helicopters with an upgraded version, the CH-53K.

Ground Combat Vehicles

The Marine Corps' plans for ground combat vehicles in the 2014 FYDP were very similar to those in the 2013 FYDP. The Marine Corps is continuing with its plan to replace the expeditionary fighting vehicle canceled in 2012. In the short term, the intention is to extend the service life of existing amphibious assault vehicles. In the longer term, the Marine Corps intends to develop and purchase a new amphibious combat vehicle, but the capabilities and quantity of that new vehicle have not yet been determined. CBO includes a rough estimate for the cost of that new vehicle in its projections.

Missiles and Munitions

Missiles and munitions encompass air-launched weapons (including air-to-air and air-to-ground missiles) and ship-launched weapons (including defensive surface-to-air missiles, land-attack missiles, and torpedoes). Notable among those weapons are a substantial number of

---

8. Instead of developing a new aircraft, the Navy might opt to purchase additional F-35Cs. That course of action would result in lower RDT&E costs than are reflected in CBO's analysis.

9. As part of the Unmanned Combat Air System Carrier Demonstration program, the Navy is developing the technologies necessary to field such aircraft. CBO's analysis reflects the assumptions that the effort will be successful and that the Navy will purchase 118 of those unmanned combat aircraft for its carrier air wings by 2028.

Figure 3-5.

Costs of the Air Force's Acquisition Plans

(Billions of 2014 dollars)

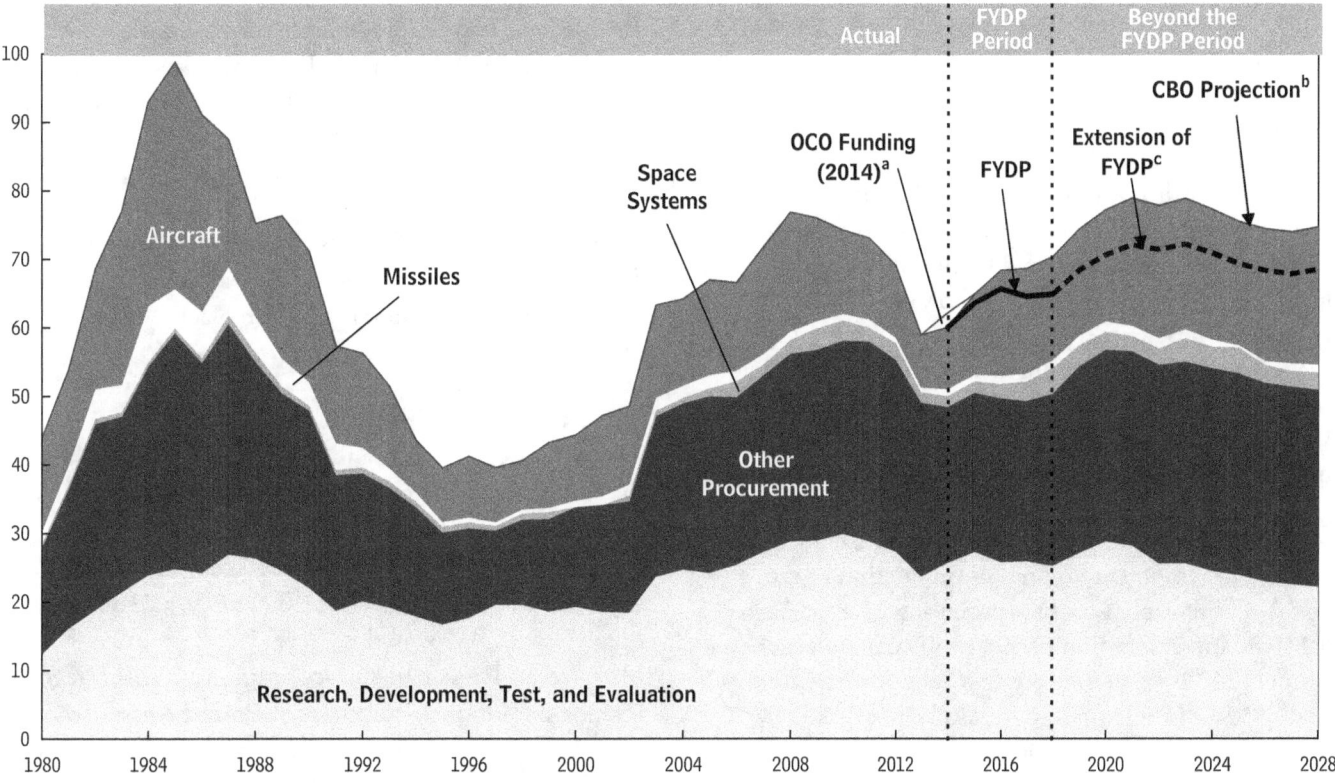

Source: Congressional Budget Office.

Notes: The amounts shown for the Future Years Defense Program (FYDP) and the extension of the FYDP are the totals for all categories.

OCO = overseas contingency operations; FYDP period = 2014 through 2018, the period for which the Department of Defense's (DoD's) plans are fully specified.

a. Supplemental and emergency funding for overseas contingency operations, such as those in Afghanistan and Iraq, is included in the individual categories for 2013 and earlier; it is shown separately for 2014 and is not included for later years.

b. Each category shows the CBO projection of the base budget from 2014 to 2028. That projection incorporates costs that are consistent with DoD's recent experience.

c. For the extension of the FYDP (2019 to 2028), CBO projects the costs of DoD's plans using the department's estimates of costs to the extent they are available and costs that are consistent with CBO's projections of price and compensation trends in the overall economy when the department's estimates are not available.

Tactical Tomahawk cruise missiles for attacking land targets and air-launched Joint Standoff Weapons, also for attacking ground targets.

The Air Force

The Air Force has requested $60 billion for acquisition in its 2014 base budget and $2.2 billion for acquisition for overseas contingency operations. According to the CBO projection of DoD's plans, the Air Force's acquisition costs would increase by 17 percent over the period of the FYDP, to $70 billion in 2018, including an 8 percent

increase between 2014 and 2015 (see Figure 3-5). Total costs for 2014 through 2018 are 4 percent higher under the CBO projection than was anticipated in the FYDP.

Beyond the FYDP period, funding for the Air Force's acquisition plans would, under the CBO projection, steadily increase to $79 billion in 2021 and then average $76 billion per year through the end of the projection period. The extension of the FYDP follows a similar pattern but has average annual costs that are 8 percent lower than the CBO projection.

For its projections of procurement costs for the Air Force, CBO tracked selected programs in three categories of major systems: aircraft, missiles and munitions, and space systems. The remaining programs are grouped together as other procurement. Funding for RDT&E is also assigned to a separate category.

Aircraft

The Air Force's plans include purchases of new aircraft and major modifications to existing aircraft. According to the CBO projection, those costs would rise significantly over the period covered by the FYDP, from $9 billion in 2014 to over $15 billion in 2018. After that, the costs of procurement of new aircraft would nearly level off for two years before increasing to an average of $19 billion per year between 2021 and 2028. The Air Force's acquisition plans for aircraft include a number of significant elements.

F-35A Joint Strike Fighter. The Air Force is continuing with the development and initial production of the F-35A. Current plans call for procuring 19 F-35As in 2014 and increasing numbers of those planes in each year through 2021, when 80 aircraft would be purchased. A total of 961 of these fighters would be purchased by 2028, and production would continue for nine years beyond that (through 2037).

KC-46A Airborne Tanker. The KC-46A is being developed by the Air Force to replace its fleet of KC-135 airborne tankers. Procurement of this new aircraft is scheduled to begin in 2015 and reach 15 aircraft per year in 2017. Current plans for the KC-46A indicate that a total of 179 tankers would be purchased, with a final 6 aircraft in 2027. The Air Force has stated, however, that replacing its entire KC-135 fleet would require additional purchases beyond the 179 planned for the KC-46A. For 2027 and 2028, therefore, CBO assumed that the Air Force would continue to purchase 15 tankers per year at costs similar to those for the KC-46A. The Air Force could, however, select a different type of aircraft (sometimes referred to as the KC-Y).

Combat Rescue Helicopter. The Air Force is implementing plans to replace its fleet of HH-60G Blackhawk helicopters with new aircraft based on an existing design. CBO's projection includes purchases of 110 such aircraft.

Long-Range Strike Bomber. The Air Force is currently reviewing performance requirements and available technologies in anticipation of developing a new long-range bomber to be fielded sometime after 2020. The 2014 FYDP posits steadily increasing annual funding for development of that system; CBO's analysis reflects the assumptions that development efforts would continue beyond the FYDP period and that procurement of this aircraft would begin in 2021. The rising cost of aircraft acquisition after 2020 would be largely due to the procurement of this aircraft.

T-X Trainer. The Air Force is currently working on defining a program to develop a new aircraft for advanced pilot training. This aircraft would replace the T-38 trainer that is in service today.

Missiles and Munitions

The Air Force's missiles and munitions include systems that range from air-to-air weapons to intercontinental ballistic missiles (ICBMs). Plans include upgrades to existing Minuteman III ICBMs to keep them in service until 2030. CBO's projections include the assumption that a new ICBM would be developed to replace the Minuteman III. Air-to-surface weapons in this category include the Joint Air-to-Surface Standoff Missile, the Joint Direct Attack Munition, and the Small-Diameter Bomb. There are also plans to field a replacement for today's Air-Launched Cruise Missile that carries a nuclear warhead.

Space Systems

Space systems consist mainly of satellites and the launch systems used to put them into orbit. In its proposed budget for 2014, the Air Force has continued acquisition initiatives that it began in the 2012 budget.

For satellite programs, the strategy (referred to as Efficient Space Procurement, or ESP) features blocks of satellites purchased at fixed prices ("block buys") combined with ongoing technology development for follow-on systems. Procurement budgets for those programs would be smoothed by spreading the cost over multiple years. In the 2014 budget, the Air Force has requested funds to continue procurement of a block of two Advanced Extremely High Frequency Satellites and a block of two Space-Based Infrared System-High satellites. For its projection, CBO assumed that the Air Force would continue to use the ESP strategy to develop and field follow-on versions of those satellites when needed.

The Air Force has also continued its efforts to improve efficiency in the procurement of the Evolved Expendable Launch Vehicle (EELV) for launching satellites. In addition to continuing block buys of EELVs with the goal of providing a more stable market for the private firms producing the EELV, the Air Force plans to increase competition for EELV acquisition by certifying new firms to provide launch services.[10] The certification process for new entrants is ongoing, and current plans call for competition for up to 14 EELV missions starting as early as 2015. In its projections, CBO assumed that EELV purchases would continue at five per year beyond the period of the FYDP.

Other Defense Activities, Including Those of the Missile Defense Agency

In addition to funding for acquisition by the Departments of the Army, Navy, and Air Force, DoD's budget includes funding for acquisition by its other components, including specialized agencies that perform advanced research, develop missile defenses, oversee special operations, and manage financial and information systems. CBO assumed that acquisition costs for defense organizations other than the Missile Defense Agency would remain constant over the course of its projection period at $16 billion—the costs for 2018 indicated in the FYDP (see Figure 3-6). For MDA, CBO has made estimates of future costs on a programmatic basis.

The 2014 budget request for MDA was $7.2 billion for acquisition ($5.6 billion for RDT&E and $1.6 billion for procurement), about $300 million for operation and maintenance, and about $200 million for military construction.[11] This section deals only with the acquisition portion of the budget; the O&M and military construction portions are included in the analysis of those

accounts in Chapters 2 and 4. According to the CBO projection of DoD's plans, which incorporates DoD's historical cost growth, MDA's acquisition costs would average $7.9 billion annually from 2014 to 2028.

The 2014 FYDP includes several major changes in individual MDA programs relative to the 2013 FYDP, with some programs having been expanded and others scaled back or canceled. The net effect is that, relative to the previous FYDP, MDA has proposed a similar budget for 2014 but somewhat smaller budgets (by 6 percent) in the years 2015 through 2017. Changes to individual programs include:

■ Expanding the Ground-Based Midcourse Defense (GMD) system, with 14 additional interceptors to be deployed to supplement the current set of 26 operational interceptors at Fort Greely in Alaska and four operational interceptors at Vandenberg Air Force Base in California. Current plans call for reallocation of existing spare and test interceptors to achieve the increase in operational capability, with procurement of new interceptors to begin in 2016 to replace the test and spare stock. As directed by the Congress, MDA is also conducting environmental impact studies regarding a possible third GMD interceptor site in the United States.

■ Halting the development of the most-advanced version of the Aegis missile defense interceptor, the SM-3 Block IIB. That interceptor, which had been slated to be available in about 2020, was intended to provide the Aegis air defense system with the ability to engage ICBMs. Although no funding for that missile is requested in the 2014 FYDP, MDA is exploring alternative approaches for an improved capability against ICBMs.

■ Canceling the Precision Tracking and Surveillance System (PTSS), a space-based system for tracking ballistic missiles and their warheads. MDA had planned to launch two initial prototype satellites in about 2017 and to begin launching an operational constellation of 6 to 12 satellites several years later, so the cancellation of PTSS would avoid about $1 billion in planned development costs during the 2014–2018 period and a larger amount in procurement costs after 2018.

---

10. In the past, EELV purchases were tied to specific satellite launches, but under the block-buy approach, boosters would be procured in lots and assigned to specific satellite launches as needed.

11. Since its inception, MDA has managed research, development, and testing of DoD's missile defense programs as components of the Ballistic Missile Defense System (BMDS). In September 2009, MDA's responsibilities were broadened to include procuring and fielding those systems in the context of the BMDS Life Cycle Management Process.

Figure 3-6.

Costs of DoD's Acquisition Plans Other Than Those for the Military Services

(Billions of 2014 dollars)

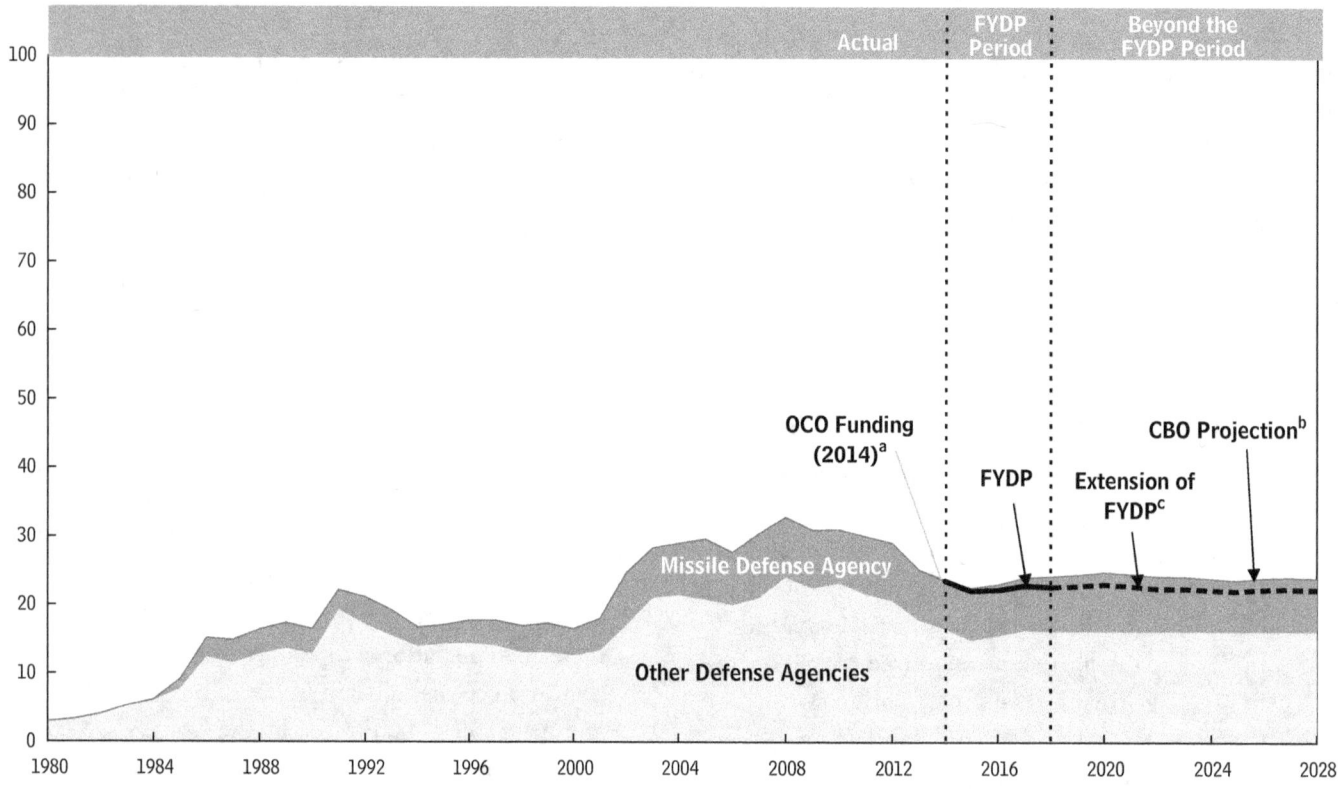

Source: Congressional Budget Office.

Notes: The amounts shown for the Future Years Defense Program (FYDP) and the extension of the FYDP are the totals for all categories.

   DoD = Department of Defense; OCO = overseas contingency operations; FYDP period = 2014 through 2018, the period for which DoD's plans are fully specified.

a.   The dollar amount for this category is $150 million. Supplemental and emergency funding for overseas contingency operations, such as those in Afghanistan and Iraq, is included in the individual categories for 2013 and earlier; it is shown separately for 2014 and is not included for later years.

b.   Each category shows the CBO projection of the base budget from 2014 to 2028. That projection incorporates costs that are consistent with DoD's recent experience.

c.   For the extension of the FYDP (2019 to 2028), CBO projects the costs of DoD's plans using the department's estimates of costs to the extent they are available and costs that are consistent with CBO's projections of price and compensation trends in the overall economy when the department's estimates are not available.